T0056717

YOUR GUIDE
TO THE
MODERN BRITISH
ROYAL FAMILY

ROYAL TRIVIA

RACHEL BOWIE
AND
ROBERTA FIORITO

Published by:
Ulysses Press
PO Box 3440
Berkeley, CA 94703
www.ulyssespress.com

ISBN: 978-1-64604-260-9
Library of Congress Catalog Number: 2021937817

Printed in the United States by Versa Press
10 9 8 7 6 5 4 3 2

Acquisitions editor: Ashten Evans
Managing editor: Claire Chun
Editor: Scott Calamar
Proofreader: Janet Vail
Front cover design: Amy King
Interior design and layout: what!design @ whatweb.com
Illustrations: cover, Amelia Noyes; interior, crown © OneLineStock
    .com/shutterstock.com
Production assistant: Yesenia Garcia

To my family, whose love and support could fill a thousand palaces, and to Dave, for becoming an unlikely royals expert.

—*Roberta*

To my mom, who introduced me to the royals via a set of Princess Diana paper dolls, and to Matt and Finn, who are now royally obsessed by default.

—*Rachel*

CONTENTS

INTRODUCTION

Rachel first fell in love with the royals via her mother. To this day, her mother claims that following every detail of Princess Diana's pregnancy with William while Rachel was still in the womb is the reason she came to be so fascinated by the royals' every move. Because even before Rachel became cohost of the podcast *Royally Obsessed* (with Roberta!), she was waiting in line to see Princess Diana's dresses (part of a traveling exhibit in 1998), shelling out big bucks to watch Kate and William sit courtside at Barclays Center, and flying to London to catch a glimpse of every palace—not just Buckingham, but Kensington and Windsor, too. Fairy-tale fantasy? Maybe. But the royals are all about an attention to detail (via their clothes, causes, and connections to each other—family drama included) and it's those subtle nods that make it a thrill to follow this modern-day monarchy in real time.

Roberta first discovered her love of all things British when her family moved to Scotland for a year. At a young age, she traveled to lochs and glens, visited castles and palaces, and realized the fairy tales piled high on her nightstand could actually be true. But her royal obsession really kicked off when Meghan Markle entered the scene nearly two decades later. A glamorous biracial American marrying into the royal family and paying tribute to her late mother-in-law, her heritage, her previous philanthropic work, American designers: it was a "Once upon a time" in real life...until it wasn't. And while the royals' evolution from archaic institution to modern monarchy comes with a bold asterisk, their every move is the stuff of history books as they navigate this uncharted territory.

Which leads us to how we came to write about the royals in trivia form. When we were first approached to write this book, trivia about the modern monarchy felt like a unique and interesting way to discuss the trajectory of our favorite royals' lives. But that's when our passion for storytelling struck.

Because to know the significance of a tidbit that's perfect for cocktail party conversations (like the fact that Princess Diana spilled her favorite perfume down her David and Elizabeth Emanuel wedding dress), you must also be able to flash back to 1981 and set the scene of the wedding of the century. When a twenty-year-old Diana walked down the aisle to marry Prince Charles at St. Paul's Cathedral, her nerves were at their peak, which is why she misspoke while saying her vows, and the pair forgot to seal "I do" with a royal kiss.

To understand the generational joy that is Prince Harry and Meghan Markle's choice to name their daughter Lilibet ("Lili") Diana after the queen and Harry's late mum, you have to know the origins of the nickname-turned-first name. In use for over nine decades, Lilibet was the result of a mispronunciation by a toddler-aged then Princess Elizabeth who struggled to enunciate her own moniker. Its use was welcomed by a royal family who adored having pet names for each other. (For example, did you know that King George V also had a nickname assigned by Elizabeth? It was Grandpa England.)

These are the details—the context behind our royal trivia questions—that we hope hook you right in. Whether you're uncovering Kate Middleton's theatrical upbringing (ahem, she played Eliza Doolittle from *My Fair Lady* at age eleven) or the fact that Princess Diana's second pregnancy announcement served as inspiration for Prince Harry and Meghan Markle for their Valentine's Day reveal, you're simultaneously getting a glimpse of the royals' evolution within the monarchy—and, in some cases, like with Harry and Meghan, life beyond it.

And that's where our own personal evolution as royal reporters (and royally obsessed fans) continues: The trajectory of this modern monarchy is still unfolding. And our book comes as we enter a time of mega milestones (from what would have been Diana's sixtieth birthday year to the queen's highly anticipated Platinum Jubilee). There are the major cultural moments—births, weddings, and funerals—that intrigue the masses and entice more royal watchers to follow along. But to know how they are all connected, how every detail is symbolic and every moment is part of a bigger history: that is why we wanted to write *Royal Trivia*. If you read each royal's story as an arc, you can immediately pinpoint the vast context, depth, and thoughtfulness of each annual event, every outfit choice, the many official royal statements, and then apply it to the modern monarchy as you, too, follow along in real time. That's why we think royal watching is so enjoyable, and why we hope you'll love reading (or playing!) with us.

PART I

THE CAMBRIDGES

Prince William's birth was hugely significant, not just because of the line of succession, but because he was the first future king to be born where?

On June 21, 1982, the world met Prince William Arthur Philip Louis Mountbatten-Windsor, born to Princess Diana and Prince Charles at 9:03 p.m. His birth was significant given that he was now officially second in line to the British throne after his father, bumping Prince Andrew, Prince Edward, and Princess Anne (who still comes after her brothers in the line of succession, regardless of birth order, due to a since-updated royal rule that placed male heirs ahead of females) down a place in the line of succession. But that's not the only thing the world was buzzing about. To mark William's arrival, Di and Charles opted to break a pretty big royal tradition—delivering him at St. Mary's Hospital in Paddington (a neighborhood in North London) and home to the now-famous Lindo Wing, instead of at Buckingham Palace. The cost of a Lindo Wing room back then was estimated to be about $230 US a day, and although the queen much preferred the idea of an at-home delivery, Charles and Di had different and more modern thoughts about birth and parenting—William's delivery location being one of the first in a vast array of royal norms they, but mainly Diana, were determined to change.

Even though William was born about ten days earlier than expected, crowds who got wind that the princess was in labor couldn't contain their excitement and gathered outside the Lindo Wing to pop champagne and sing "For He's a Jolly Good Fellow." A more formal announcement was posted on the gates of Buckingham Palace.

Diana later revealed to journalist Andrew Morton, author of *Diana: Her True Story* with a secret assist from the princess herself, that the pressure around William's birth, in particular with the media, became too much to bear, so much so that she asked her doctors to induce labor. She was in labor for thirteen hours with Charles by her side the whole time. When Charles finally emerged from the hospital close to midnight, he remarked that William was "lucky enough" not to look like him. He added that the experience was "rather a grown-up thing, I find, rather a shock to my system."

Diana, who gave birth to William just shy of her twenty-first birthday on July 1, was pictured out and about right up until William was born. She attended the Royal Ascot, an event best described by *Town & Country* as a "cross between a royal wedding and the Kentucky Derby," only the week before, then drove her own car to greet Charles as he returned home from France just a handful of days before William's arrival.

Growing up, Prince William had a playful nickname bestowed on him by Princess Diana that's stuck with him over time. What was it?

Although he's said to go by Wills around close friends and was rumored to use the pseudonym "Steve" at the University of St. Andrews to maintain some level of anonymity, William revealed in an interview on NBC back in 2007 that there's another nickname he goes by to this day that's as silly as it is beloved. When he was just a baby, the young prince embarked on his first—and now infamous, thanks to *The Crown* —royal tour to Australia with Princess Diana and Prince Charles. Not long after that trip, Diana assigned him another moniker that she and Charles both used interchangeably with his name: Willie the Wombat. In the conversation with NBC, William explains: "When we went to Australia with our parents, and the wombat, you know, that's the local animal, so I just basically got called that. Not because I look like a wombat... or maybe I do." He added, "I can't get rid of it now. It began when I was two."

That wasn't the only nickname given to Prince William as a young boy. During his nursery school years at Jane Mynors' Nursery School—located just a five-minute walk from Kensington Palace—he was known to be a bit of a terror, getting into playground skirmishes and squabbles with his classmates. This earned him the nickname "Basher Billy," something Diana was keen to put a stop to at an early age. Diana's former bodyguard, Ken Wharfe, revealed in an interview that the Princess of Wales told William: "Future king of England or not, I will not hesitate to put your kingly bum in a timeout!" (There were also quite a few eyebrows raised about his behavior at the age of four, given Diana and Charles's interest in a more liberal upbringing for their boys.) In reference to William's nickname, Diana once compared her boys: "William's very enthusiastic about things. He pushes himself right into it. Harry is quieter and just watches. No. 2 skates in quite nicely. But the bad luck about being No. 1 is trial and error, so we're open-minded about William."

Prince William originally enrolled at the University of St. Andrews to study art history. What major did he pivot to instead?

After nursery school, William went on to attend the pre-preparatory Wetherby School, then Ludgrove School and Eton College. (The choice to send William—and eventually Prince Harry—to Eton was a big deal in that it went against the royal family's tradition of attending Gordonstoun in Scotland, a school both Prince Philip and Prince Charles had gone to.

Instead, it was Diana's father, the 8th Earl Spencer, and brother, Charles Spencer, who had been educated at Eton, paving the way for William to attend.) But post-Eton and following a gap year, William enrolled in 2001 at the University of St. Andrews in Scotland—another break in royal tradition since, for the past 150 years, royals either went to Oxford or Cambridge Universities. His original focus was art history, but after a short stint studying that as his main subject, he switched to geography, graduating in 2005 with a Scottish master's degree (the equivalent of a bachelor's degree in the US) and upper second class honors. This meant that, academically, William outperformed both Prince Charles and Prince Edward at school. (Charles and Edward both attended Cambridge.)

Graduation is, of course, a milestone moment all its own, but for Prince William, there was added significance as it meant the end of an agreement made with the British media not to intrude into the prince's private life during his time as a student. (This arrangement came to be in 1997, following the death of Princess Diana in a car crash while she was being aggressively chased by paparazzi.)

Kate Middleton was born in Berkshire, England, but she spent two and a half years in which Middle Eastern country?

*C*atherine Elizabeth Middleton (or Kate, as we like to call her) was born on January 9, 1982, to Carole and Michael Middleton at the Royal Berkshire Hospital in Reading, England. Just like her future husband, Prince William, Kate is the firstborn. (Her sister, Philippa Charlotte, who goes by Pippa, arrived in September 1983, and her brother, James, followed in April 1987.) Kate grew up in Reading, England, a small town located about fifty miles west of London. Her parents now own an $8 million, seven-bedroom home called Bucklebury Manor—but her father's job as an aero manager for British Airways took Kate and her family to Amman, the capital of Jordan, for two and a half years beginning in May 1984. (They moved back to England in September 1986.) While there, Kate attended an English-language nursery school and, according to an interview with Carole in the *Telegraph*, her family lived a comfortable life. Still, she said at a certain point she was ready to move back: "I wasn't convinced I wanted to be an expat mum and Mike's job was coming to an end."

Kate Middleton has always been athletic, but what other childhood hobby was she known to excel at?

*T*heater! Yes, during Kate's time at Marlborough College, an elite boarding school, she was captain of the field hockey team and participated in other sports. But as a student at St. Andrew's School (not to be confused with the University of St. Andrews) in Pangbourne, a place she attended from age four until thirteen, she starred in two of the school's theatrical productions: *My Fair Lady* and a Victorian melodrama called *Murder in the Red Barn*. A testament to her talents on stage? She even played the lead in *My Fair Lady*, stepping into the shoes of Eliza Doolittle. (It's worth a Google—there's video footage on YouTube of an eleven-year-old Kate belting out "Wouldn't It Be Loverly?" in her school production.)

Vocal talents aside, Kate revealed more about her idyllic childhood on the *Happy Mum, Happy Baby* podcast in early 2020: "I had an amazing granny who devoted a lot of time to us, playing with us, doing arts and crafts, and going to the green-house to do gardening, and cooking with us," she explained.

Kate Middleton's parents met while working for British Airways, but both eventually quit their jobs to prioritize a burgeoning business idea of Carole's. What was it?

*W*hen Kate's parents returned from Amman, Carole and Michael decided to throw caution to the wind and start their own mail-order party-supply company, called Party Pieces. The goal was for Carole to be able to quit her job working as a flight attendant for British Airways (a career that led her to meet Michael), but she was in her early thirties and had bills to pay. She came up with the idea for a one-stop shop for busy "mums" prepping for children's parties and launched it, working out of her home in Bucklebury, in 1987 (the same year James was born).

What kicked off with a self-designed flyer that she posted at Kate's local play group is now a multimillion-dollar family business. According to a piece in the *Telegraph*, as recently as 2018, Party Pieces had a staff of thirty and was dispatching around four thousand orders a week during busy seasons. Kate was even known to lend a hand, according to Carole. In that same article in the *Telegraph*, Carole revealed: "[Party Pieces] was part of the children's lives—it still is—and they'd come and help. They did a lot of modeling. Catherine was on the cover of one of the catalogues, blowing out candles. Later on, she did some styling and set up the First Birthday side of the business. Pippa did the blog." In fact, as late as 2010, Kate was penning articles for the website with a byline that read simply "Kate from Party Pieces," although that content was subsequently taken down.

Carole and Michael's success running Party Pieces is said to have paved the way for Kate's education at Marlborough, a fancy boarding school whose alumni also include Princess Eugenie, Prince William's cousin and the youngest daughter of Prince Andrew and Sarah, the Duchess of York. After transferring there halfway through her second year of school, Kate struggled to find her footing at first but eventually hit her stride, joining the field hockey team, picking up the clarinet, serving as a prefect, and more. After that, she was off to the University of St. Andrews in Fife, Scotland, where fate would intervene.

Prince William was said to be especially close with his mother, Princess Diana. How did her death at age thirty-six impact his life?

William was just fifteen years old when his mother, Diana, was killed in a car crash in the Pont de l'Alma tunnel in Paris on August 31, 1997. He described the impact on his life in the HBO documentary *Diana, Our Mother: Her Life and Legacy*: "Slowly, you try to rebuild your life, you try to understand what happened. I kept myself busy, as well, to allow you to get yourself through that initial shock phase. We're talking maybe as much as five to seven years afterwards." In fact, the experience of walking behind her coffin during her ceremonial funeral is something William has described as "one of the hardest things I've ever done."

Still, William—along with his younger brother, Prince Harry—was subjected to Diana's efforts to introduce them to more normal (read: real) sides of life from a young age. She took them to McDonald's and amusement parks and even made the young princes wait their turn in line for various rides. But she also made sure that William and Harry knew what the lives of others looked like via visits to homeless shelters, taking London's subway (the Tube), and more. William revealed in an interview on ABC: "[My mother] very much wanted to get us to see the rawness of real life. And I can't thank her enough for that because reality bites in a big way and it was one of the biggest lessons I learned—just how lucky and privileged so many of us are—particularly myself."

After Diana died, William made it his mission to continue her humanitarian work. After graduating from Eton in 2000, he embarked on a gap year in which he traveled to Belize with the Welsh Guard, worked on a dairy farm, and went to Kenya,

Botswana, Tanzania, and Chile to do charity work. "I wanted to do something constructive. I thought this was a way of trying to help people out and meet a whole range of different people," he later said of that time.

Although Prince William and Kate Middleton were both students at the University of St. Andrews, what on-campus event is said to have piqued William's interest in Kate?

*I*t's true that William and Kate both kicked off their education at the University of St. Andrews with a focus on art history. (William later changed to geography while Kate graduated in 2005 with a degree in art history.) They also shared a residence hall—St. Salvator's—and are said to have bumped into each other frequently in the stairwell there. (Kate said in their engagement interview in 2010: "I actually went bright red when I met you and scuttled off feeling very shy about meeting you.") Still, it wasn't until 2002 when William witnessed Kate—famous for being shy—walking the runway in a charity fashion show that his romantic interest ignited.

The young prince—who had hesitated about returning to St. Andrews for a second semester after feeling a bit daunted about being away from home, as well as not loving his art history track (Kate is said to have been the one who convinced him to stay at the school)—had paid £200 for his front-row seat at the "Don't Walk" charity event. Kate appeared in a see-through dress, and William was caught off guard. Up until this point, they'd both been dating other people, and William considered Kate to be a good friend. (The pair supposedly sat together for breakfast in the dining hall, swam together most mornings, and would meet for drinks in their dorm's common room after a rigorous day of classes.)

The fashion show—and the after-party—is the moment everything changed for the pair. In the darkly lit room, William is rumored to have made the first move. Friends who witnessed their interaction said they were huddled in a quiet corner, chatting, before William leaned in for a kiss—and one that Kate actually declined. As their friends told *Vanity Fair*, "[William] actually told [Kate] she was a knockout that night, which caused her to blush. There was definitely chemistry between them, and Kate had really made an impression on William. She played it very cool, and at one point when William seemed to lean in to kiss her, she pulled away. She didn't want to give off the wrong impression or make it too easy for Will."

Kate Middleton and Prince William dated for nearly ten years before getting engaged. But they also broke up for a brief period of time. Why?

*A*lthough their courtship wasn't made public until 2004, Kate and William were living together beginning in their second year of school at St. Andrews. As William later described in his engagement interview: "We lived with a couple of others as well, and [our relationship] just sort of blossomed from there really." But in 2004, they were spotted on the ski slopes together in the Swiss village of Klosters, and the tabloid the *Sun* confirmed their royal romance with the headline: "Finally...Wills Gets a Girl." By 2006, Kate was given her own twenty-four-hour security detail, and the pair went on to share numerous milestones and occasions together—their graduation from St. Andrews in 2005, William's graduation from the Royal Military Academy Sandhurst in 2006 (a priority for him, but also a necessity ahead of his service with the Blues and Royals, entry into the Royal Air Force College Cranwell, and subsequent career in the RAF Search and Rescue Force), and a lot of weddings. (The one that had the press all aflutter was Kate's attendance at the nuptials of Camilla Parker Bowles's daughter, Laura, in 2006.)

Still, the pair parted ways for a few months in early 2007 after William broke things off. The announcement of their split came at the same time the *Spectator* had dubbed Kate "the next People's Princess," an homage to Princess Diana. But that was part of the problem: The pressure on William to propose was on. According to reports, William—who'd dated Kate since 2002—began to have doubts about their relationship. Kate wasn't happy about the split, but while William was photographed partying with other girls, she refocused on herself, signing up for the Sisterhood, a group of women who planned to row a dragon boat all the way from Dover, England, to Cap Gris-Nez, near Calais in France, for charity. But before the race took place, Kate and William were back together. (She was photographed seated just a couple of rows behind him, with her sister Pippa, at the Princess Diana tribute concert in July of 2007.)

It's also worth noting that this wasn't Kate and William's first split. According to royal biographer Katie Nicholl, the pair spent time apart just ahead of their St. Andrews graduation, as well, something William addressed in their engagement interview with Tom Bradby for ITV in 2010: "We were both very young. It was at university, we were sort of both finding ourselves. It was very much trying to find our own way and we were growing up and so it was a bit of space...and things worked out for the better."

Kate also spoke of the breaks in their relationship: "At the time, I wasn't very happy about it. But it made me a stronger person. You find out things about yourself that maybe you hadn't realized. I think you can get quite consumed by a relationship when you're younger. I really valued that time for me." William also explained that the early stumbling blocks in their courtship are what ultimately led their partnership to feel so solid in the long run.

Upon their engagement announcement, what did Prince William reveal about his proposal in their engagement interview?

*O*n November 16, 2010, it was official: Kate and William were engaged. Both twenty-eight years old at the time, it was revealed that Prince William sought both the permission of the queen, but also Kate's father, Michael Middleton, after he popped the question to Kate. ("If I asked Kate first, I thought [Mike] couldn't really say no," he joked during his interview with ITV.)

The news put an end to the merciless tabloid headline, "Waity Katie," and the will he/won't he narrative that was playing out in the press. It also brought about the reemergence of one of the most iconic engagement rings of all time: Diana's twelve-carat oval Ceylon sapphire that's surrounded with fourteen solitaire diamonds. There, in plain sight on Kate's finger during their announcement, was the ring. William explained in their engagement interview that giving the ring to Kate was his way of "making sure my mother didn't miss out on today and the excitement." He added: "It's very special to me. As Kate's very special to me now, it was right to put the two together." (It was later revealed that Prince Harry had actually been the one to inherit Diana's engagement ring upon her death in 1997, while William received his mother's gold Cartier Tank Française watch, but Harry offered to swap the watch with William so he could use the ring for his proposal to Kate.)

As for how he proposed, William told Tom Bradby in the engagement interview that he popped the question a few weeks prior to their official announcement while on holiday in Kenya with some friends. He acknowledged that it wasn't a total surprise, as they'd been talking about marriage for quite some time at that point, but he had been nervously carrying his mother's ring around in his rucksack for going on three weeks and feeling like he'd have a lot to answer for if the ring got lost. Kate added that the whole thing was very romantic—but also caught her off guard. "We were out with friends and things so I really didn't expect it all," she revealed in her engagement interview. "I thought he might have maybe thought about it, but no. It was a total shock when it came and very excited [sic]."

The pair have a ton in common — a love of sports, but also cooking. What other interests do Kate Middleton and Prince William share?

A shared enthusiasm for athletics might be Kate and William's most well-known couple trait. William plays polo, tennis, and rugby, while Kate does well at tennis, field hockey, swimming, and more. Throughout their courtship, some of their more endearing public moments together have taken place on (and off) the field, for example, when they both tried their hand at bow-and-arrow practice while on tour in 2016 in Bhutan or when they (along with Prince Harry) raced against each other in 2017 at a London Marathon training session to promote their mental health organization, Heads Together. That's not all: While sitting courtside at events ranging from Wimbledon to a trip to watch the Brooklyn Nets basketball team play while on a tour of the US in 2014, it's near impossible not to see their obvious enthusiasm. (Like anyone could forget their spontaneous PDA during a cycling event at the London 2012 Summer Olympics.)

But that's not the only thing they have in common: During an event with Mary Berry at the end of 2019, they both showed off their skill in the kitchen with Kate revealing that William spent much of their courtship wooing her with home-cooked meals. She also referenced William's famous bolognese sauce, made from tomatoes, minced beef, garlic, wine, and herbs. "In our university days, he used to cook all sorts of meals. I think that's when he was trying to impress me," she told the former *Great British Bake Off* host. William chimed in to say that, while he's an expert at making tea, Kate now handles most of the culinary efforts at home. (They also are prone to order takeout, according to an interview they did with BBC Radio 1 in 2017: As long as it's not too spicy—William's words—Indian food is a top choice for the pair.)

Kate and William also seem to have a similar sense of humor. At engagements, they're often laughing and sharing inside jokes. Their banter is on full display in their engagement video when Tom Bradby teases Kate about the rumor that she had a poster of Prince William on her wall when she was younger. William instantly responds: "There wasn't just one [photo], there were ten...twenty!" Kate's sarcastic reply: "He wishes. No, I had the Levi's guy on my wall, not a picture of William. Sorry." Still, William can't let it go by, adding: "It was me in Levi's. Obviously."

The Cambridges' wedding date was named a national holiday in the UK. What was Kate Middleton's "something old, something new, something borrowed, and something blue," as tradition goes?

*W*hen hundreds of millions of people tuned in from around the world to watch Kate and William wed on April 29, 2011, attention was on the nuptials, sure, but more importantly, the world would finally get the answer to the question: Who designed Kate's dress? Speculation was at an all-time high. There were even claims that Kate had commissioned not one, but three wedding dress options. But mum was the word from St. James's Palace: "Miss Middleton is keen to keep one secret for the wedding day itself," a statement read.

Still, St. James's Palace had the confirmation the minute Kate stepped out of the Rolls-Royce Phantom VI to walk down the aisle at Westminster Abbey in front of two thousand cellphone-less guests on the arm of her father, Michael Middleton. The dress—which was Victorian-inspired—was created by Sarah Burton for Alexander McQueen, and Kate worked closely with Burton on the design of the dress. A statement from the palace also revealed: "Miss Middleton chose British brand Alexander McQueen for the beauty of its craftsmanship and its respect for traditional workmanship and the technical construction of clothing." It went on to discuss Kate's desire to combine "tradition and modernity"—in other words, this choice was her "something old." (The handmade lace technique on the sleeves and bodice, called traditional Carrickmacross craftsmanship, dates back to the 1800s. The motif—in the shapes of a rose, a thistle, a daffodil, and a shamrock to represent England, Scotland, Wales, and Northern Ireland respectively— was carried out by the Royal School of Needlework.)

For Kate's "something new," she chose a pair of pendant earrings, designed by Robinson Pelham and gifted to her on her wedding day by her parents, which featured stylized oak leaves and diamond pavé acorns—a nod to the Middleton family's coat of arms. Something borrowed? That one was easy: the 1936 Cartier Halo Tiara, on loan from the queen. (For reference, this tiara was purchased by Queen Elizabeth II's father, King George VI, for his wife, Queen Elizabeth at the time. He bought it just a few weeks before he succeeded his brother, Edward VIII, who voluntarily abdicated as king. The tiara was then gifted to then Princess Elizabeth on her eighteenth birthday.) Kate's "something blue" was a nod to her late mother-in-law, Princess Diana. She asked Sarah Burton to sew a blue ribbon into the interior of her dress for good luck, just as Diana had secretly sewn one into hers back in 1981. (Some even say that it was the same ribbon from Diana's dress, although this hasn't been confirmed.)

One major detail that drew gasps from the crowd: Kate's wedding train. At nearly nine feet long, it made for a gorgeously dramatic entrance to the abbey, in particular the moment that Kate's sister, Pippa Middleton—also wearing Sarah Burton by Alexander McQueen, extended it out to its full length for the world to see. (By comparison, Princess Diana's train was twenty-five feet in length.)

As for Prince William, it was hard not to draw parallels to Prince Charming. He wore the bright red coat of an Irish Guards mounted officer, appropriate given his senior honorary military role.

The royal wedding was rumored to have cost a whopping $34 million. Most of that went to security, but the flower budget was estimated to be a large piece of that financial pie. How much?

*A*ccording to reports, Kate and William spent approximately $800,000 on Shane Connolly & Company, the florist hired for their wedding. But that expense didn't just cover Kate's bouquet, which included hyacinth, lily of the valley, myrtle, and sweet William (a romantic tribute to her future spouse), it covered the cost of the English field maples that lined the aisle of Westminster Abbey—trees that were

ROYAL TRIVIA

later replanted at Prince Charles's vacation home in Wales. As for the myrtle featured in Kate's bridal arrangement, that was plucked from the very same plant used in Queen Elizabeth II's wedding bouquet in 1947, a tradition that dates back to Queen Victoria's reign. (The original bush was planted in her garden in 1846.)

Other expenses: Kate's Alexander McQueen dress is said to have come in at just around $434,000, while Kate and William's cakes were estimated at $80,000 each. (One was an eight-tier fruitcake, prepared by baker Fiona Cairns to include a multitude of details—flowers symbolizing the four nations of the United Kingdom; an oak and acorn, which is emblematic of endurance; and more sweet William, which is said to represent gallantry, bravery, and finesse. The groom's cake was chocolate biscuit, said to be a family recipe and a Prince William favorite.)

Security made up the largest part, estimated to cost approximately $32 million. But there were a couple of details that helped keep the cost down. For one thing, the piece of Welsh gold used to fashion Kate's wedding band was gifted to William by the queen. (Prince William doesn't wear a wedding ring, a matter of "personal preference," St. James's Palace confirmed in 2011.) Kate also did her own makeup for the big day, following at least a week's worth of makeup lessons courtesy of London-based makeup artist Arabella Preston.

The wedding was followed by a luncheon and formal dinner hosted by the queen and Prince Charles, but who was in charge of the after-party?

$\mathcal{F}$ollowing their wedding at Westminster Abbey, a horse-drawn carriage ride around London, and a public photo op on the Buckingham Palace balcony, the private celebrations began, including a luncheon hosted by William's grandmother, Queen Elizabeth II, at Buckingham Palace. Just over six hundred guests scored invites to the celebration. Immediately following, the newlyweds departed the palace for Clarence House to prep for their nighttime reception—hosted at Buckingham Palace by Charles and said to be much more intimate with just three hundred guests—in Charles's Aston Martin, customized with balloons and a "JU5T WED" license plate. (Fun fact: Prince Harry was in charge of decorating their getaway car and, in addition to the balloons and streamers, decided to prank Prince William by attaching a UK learner's permit sticker, which according to royal expert Myka Meier, usually inspires everyone you drive by to honk and wave.)

But about that reception… Kate changed out of her wedding dress and into a less formal strapless dress and angora-wool bolero jacket, also designed by Sarah Burton for Alexander

McQueen. William swapped his Irish Guards uniform for a tux. The night kicked off with a three-course dinner prepped by chef Anton Mosimann (a leaked menu revealed courses ranging from herb-stuffed Welsh lamb to honeycomb ice cream). But it was Prince Harry who surprised the crowds when, post-dinner, he led guests into the Throne Room at the palace, which had been transformed into a nightclub. British pop singer Ellie Goulding took the mic while Kate and William kicked things off with their first dance to Goulding's rendition of Elton John's "Your Song." (Goulding later told *Vogue* that, during her performance, she was so nervous, her hands were shaking.) The celebrations continued until 2:30 a.m., when guests were ushered into the courtyard for a fireworks display.

Although the pair left Buckingham Palace the next morning in a private helicopter, William was work bound, set to return to Wales and his job with the Royal Air Force after a long weekend with Kate. (They eventually departed for a two-week honeymoon on a private island in the Seychelles, just off the coast of Africa.)

What did the Duke and Duchess of Cambridge do at their wedding to honor Prince William's late mother, Princess Diana?

While reports claim that Kate and William made a trip to the Althorp Estate a week ahead of their wedding date to lay flowers at Princess Diana's final resting place on an island in Oval Lake and wander the estate, they also incorporated many tributes to William's late mother throughout their wedding day.

Beyond Kate's "something blue"—a blue ribbon sewn into the interior of her dress just as Diana had done—William was said to have greeted Diana's eldest sister, Lady Sarah McCorquodale, first upon his arrival to the chapel. (For her part, Lady Sarah wore the very same earrings that Diana wore when she wed Charles in 1981, a tribute to Diana on her son's wedding day.)

William and Kate also asked Richard Chartres, the Bishop of London, a trustee who presided over Princess Diana's will, to deliver their wedding address. They selected "Guide Me, O Thou Great Redeemer," as a wedding hymn—a song that also happened to be the final selection sung at Diana's funeral in 1997. Additional tributes: Elton John, who was a dear friend of Princess Diana and who performed "Candle in the Wind" at her funeral, was on the guest list. Kate, just like Diana, opted to omit the word "obey" from her vows.

The final nod? A balcony kiss post-wedding at Buckingham Palace. Just as Charles had been urged to do for the first time ever in royal history by crowds back in 1981, Prince William kissed Kate not once, but twice. The only thing that upstaged this moment was Grace van Cutsem, their flower girl who, less than pleased with the deafening noise from the crowds, looked a touch disgruntled and clapped both her hands over her ears.

What titles did Kate Middleton and Prince William pick up on their wedding day?

Up until William wed Kate, he was known as Prince William of Wales. Upon his marriage, William became the Duke of Cambridge; Kate the Duchess of Cambridge. William also was given the title of the Earl of Strathearn (a region of Scotland, not far from where he met Kate at St. Andrews), which he uses when he visits Scotland, and Baron Carrickfergus (a region in Northern Ireland), his official Irish title. With these additions, he now has three hereditary titles, reflective of three of the four countries of the United Kingdom. It's the same for Kate: she's known as the Countess of Strathearn and Baroness Carrickfergus when she visits those respective regions.

Prince William and Kate Middleton spent the first two years of marriage living on a remote island in Wales, called Anglesey. Why?

A small island off the northwest tip of Wales, Anglesey is known for its low-key way of life, expansive beaches, and fifty-eight-character Welsh name (not kidding, it's Llanfairpwllgwyngyllgogerychwyrndrobwllllantysiliogogogoch). It's also the place where William was stationed with the Royal Air Force leading up to and for the first two years of his marriage to Kate. (Kate supposedly was a frequent visitor before the wedding, but only moved in—and got rid of her London flat—after their wedding.)

Locals were said to be very protective of the royal duo, granting them a great amount of privacy while they got their footing ahead of a return to London and a much more public life. That was also made easier by the location of their home—a four-bedroom farmhouse in the Welsh-speaking hamlet of Bodorgan that they rented from a local landowner (and longtime friend of the family) for about £750 a month. During their days there, Kate was spotted several times at the local supermarket; William often went out for jogs, chatting with locals along the way. They both were seen at the movie theater catching films like *The Inbetweeners* and *Toy Story 3* and were even reported to spend their time pheasant shooting and surfing, too.

That all came to an end after the birth of Prince George on July 22, 2013, and the official conclusion of Prince William's search-and-rescue tour with the RAF. Ahead of their September departure, it surprised many that Kate was spotted on the island only a handful of weeks after George's arrival. (Carole Middleton even stayed for weeks at a time to help with the care of George, with Kate later revealing that a newborn baby in combination with William's night shifts had left her feeling "isolated" on the island as a new mom.) Still, at one of William's final events on the island, he remarked: "I know that I speak for Catherine when I say that I have never in my life known somewhere as beautiful and as welcoming as Anglesey."

Kate Middleton is a royal style icon: her outfit choices are said to have bolstered the UK fashion economy by nearly £1 billion. Who is her longtime stylist and friend?

*I*t's true: Kate is one of the most stylish members of the royal family. But the credit goes to her beloved stylist and friend, Natasha Archer (who, psst, just so happens to be married to Chris Jackson, the Getty photographer responsible for many a royal portrait including Prince Charles's seventieth birthday shots). In fact, Natasha—who started out as a personal assistant to Kate—is so good at her job, she was invested with the Royal Victorian Order in 2019 for her services. (Kate was appointed Dame Grand Cross of the Royal Victorian Order that same year.)

Archer was famously spotted arriving at the Lindo Wing back in 2013, hours after it was announced that Kate had given birth to Prince George. A short time later, Kate appeared on the front steps, dressed in her iconic blue-and-white polka-dot Jenny Packham dress, George in her arms. (Credit goes to Natasha for that outfit.) Beyond that, she's famously helped the Duchess of Cambridge evolve her style over the course of her marriage to Prince William. Although she has worked at the palace since 2007, she joined Kate's style team in 2014 and managed her transition away from A-line dresses and nude pumps into the style icon she's gradually become. She's also shadowed Kate on many a royal tour, and was said to have hiked six hours with her to a Bhutan monastery, just in case Kate needed a wardrobe change ahead of meeting photographers at the top.

While Archer remains Kate's main stylist, recently she's enlisted the expertise of others, mainly Ginnie Chadwyck-Healey, a former fashion editor at *Vogue*, who helped sub in while Natasha took maternity leave in late 2018.

Which dress launched "the Kate Effect" and how has that changed the royals' impact on fashion?

*W*hen Kate and William announced their engagement, there was Kate, wearing a $600 dark-blue dress from Issa London. It sold out in twenty-four hours and even led to a spike in the search term "little blue dress." Thus began the "Kate Effect," aka Kate's ability to put under-the-radar designers on the map. But it went far beyond that: yes, Kate is known to sport high-end designers like Alexander McQueen (hello, her wedding dress), Jenny Packham, and Chanel, but it's her ability to mix in off-the-rack styles that has kept her approach to fashion feeling not only relatable but attainable.

For example, when Kate wore a Seraphine maternity dress in 2013 for her first official portrait with Prince George, the brand's sales went up 400 percent. Ditto anything she picks up from places like Zara, Topshop, ASOS, or Reiss. Instagram (which actually launched a month before Kate and William announced they were engaged) only upped the ante on Kate's sartorial power, giving all who follow her the ability to instantly shop, in particular thanks to fan accounts like WhatKateWore and more. This not only applies to Kate, but also to other royals—and their children. It's the Trotters jumper worn by

Prince Louis in his birthday portraits, the Rothy's flats worn by Meghan Markle on her Australian tour. Bottom line: clothes (and the message they send, be it about price point or sustainability) are a big part of royal duty.

Kate Middleton has a slew of royal patronages, but which one is the most near and dear to her heart...and also an amateur hobby of hers?

*K*ate's affinity for photography—and her role in capturing casual shots of her family, specifically the kids—has become a celebrated hobby, but also one that puts her in control of the narrative. The shots of George, Charlotte, and Louis shared on Instagram are often ones she snapped herself to mark occasions ranging from birthdays to first days of school to lockdown crafts. (That rainbow finger painting DIY demonstrated by Prince Louis was replicated by so many during the COVID-19 pandemic.) Her skills as a go-to photographer for her family were even more prominent following the death of Prince Philip—Kate's photo of the Queen and Philip surrounded by seven of their great-grandchildren from 2018 is now iconic. (Scroll through @theroyalfamily on Instagram to see it.)

But she's put her skills to good use for a cause, as well. In 2020, Kate photographed Holocaust survivors and their descendants for an exhibition marking the seventy-fifth anniversary of the end of the World War II genocide. And during the heart of the pandemic—the summer of 2020—she worked closely with the National Portrait Gallery (one of her royal patronages) to launch a national campaign, called "Hold Still," which invited anyone in the UK to share a snap of what their lives looked like during COVID-19.

The initiative received more than thirty thousand submissions—photos of hospital staffers, families coping with homeschooling, and people communicating with loved ones through windows. The Duchess herself helped narrow the submissions down to one hundred winners, displayed in a virtual gallery and all around London. The final one hundred were also turned into a coffee-table book called *Hold Still: A Portrait of Our Nation in 2020* with a forward by Kate and proceeds going to the National Portrait Gallery and the mental health charity Mind.

Kate Middleton and Prince William's first royal tour as a married couple was to North America. Where did they visit?

*I*n late June 2011, the Duke and Duchess of Cambridge, still newlyweds, were Canada- and California-bound for an eleven-day royal tour, which marked their first trip together as a married couple. (It was also Kate's first time visiting both Canada and the US.) The trip was set up to be a whirlwind. The duo visited seven Canadian cities in just over seven days before jetting off for a long weekend in Los Angeles, then flying home to the UK.

The trip was a huge success, with William and Kate making headlines for visiting a tree that was planted by Princess Diana and Prince Charles in Ottawa, then planting another one; posing with *Anne of Green Gables* characters (a favorite childhood book for Kate) at the author's real address on Prince Edward Island; and competing against each other in a dragon boat race, again, out on Prince Edward Island.

From there, they were off to California, touching down in Los Angeles for a series of private events including a charity polo match (William participated!) to benefit the American Friends of the Foundation of Prince William and Prince Harry, and an appearance at the inaugural British Academy of Film and Television Arts "Brits to Watch" bash alongside A-listers including Nicole Kidman and Tom Hanks at the Belasco theater. (William, who is still president of BAFTA, gave a speech, while Kate shined by his side in a lilac Alexander McQueen gown, her go-to.)

As for the reception the Duke and Duchess of Cambridge received, Stephen Fry, who was one of three hundred guests in attendance at the BAFTA event, best summed it up: "If you brought Clark Gable and Marilyn Monroe back to life, America wouldn't be more excited than they are by the presence of the Cambridges," reported the *Telegraph*.

Kate Middleton first announced she was pregnant with Prince George in December 2012. Why did the announcement from St. James's Palace come earlier than expected?

*I*t was December 2012, and just about a year and a half since their royal wedding, when news broke that the Duchess of Cambridge (thirty years old at the time) was expecting a baby— her first!—with Prince William. But, with Kate not yet twelve weeks pregnant, the formal announcement was a surprise. The statement from St. James's Palace explained: "The Duchess was admitted this afternoon to King Edward VII Hospital in Central London with hyperemesis gravidarum. As the pregnancy is in its very early stages, Her Royal Highness is expected to stay in hospital for several days and will require a period of rest there-after." In other words, Kate was suffering from severe morning sickness (something she later experienced during the pregnancies of Princess Charlotte and Prince Louis, too).

A hospital stay made it possible for her to receive supplemental hydration and nutrients, so with William by her side, she was admitted for a few days before returning home to rest at Kensington Palace. At the time, speculation that Kate and William would announce an heir to the throne on the way was rampant—and ongoing from the moment they said "I do," hence the Cambridges' efforts to get ahead of the press who no doubt would catch wind of their hospital stay.

Kate later revealed in an interview with *Happy Mum, Happy Baby* podcast host Giovanna Fletcher in January 2020 that her experience with morning sickness each round was grueling. "[It was] utterly rotten," the Duchess of Cambridge explained. "I was really sick. I wasn't eating the things I should be eating, and yet the body was still able to take all the goodness from my body and grow new life, which I think is fascinating."

Back to the royal announcement: Beyond mentioning Kate's acute morning sickness, the announcement also made clear how thrilled the royal family was by this news. "The Queen, the Duke of Edinburgh, the Prince of Wales, the Duchess of Cornwall and Prince Harry and members of both families are delighted," the statement read.

Kate Middleton and Prince William are now mum and dad to Prince George, Princess Charlotte, and Prince Louis. What do we know about each of those royal births?

*P*rince William and Kate Middleton welcomed Prince George Alexander Louis of Cambridge on July 22, 2013, at 4:24 p.m. He was born in the Lindo Wing of St. Mary's Hospital and weighed 8 pounds and 6 ounces. They even waited four hours before sharing the news with the world, so they had a bit of time to spend with their baby first, according to a palace aide. (It also gave them time to phone the queen and their families to share the happy news.) The word of George's arrival finally came at 8:29 p.m., via an easel outside Buckingham Palace, per tradition, that read: "The Duchess of Cambridge has been delivered of a son." Kate exited St. Mary's Hospital a day later, Prince George in her arms and Prince William by her side, wearing a cornflower-blue polka-dot dress designed by Jenny Packham, a nod to Princess Diana who also wore a dot print (her dress was green) on the Lindo Wing steps when Prince William arrived in 1982. (Kate also got a lot of credit for not hiding her postpartum belly—and subsequently busting a pregnancy taboo.)

Princess Charlotte Elizabeth Diana of Cambridge was next (with a name that nodded to both her great-grandmother Queen Elizabeth II and her late grandmother Princess Diana), arriving on May 2, 2015, at 8:34 a.m. and delivered at the Lindo Wing, just like her older brother. She weighed 8 pounds and 3 ounces. This time, tradition changed: Prince William and Kate Middleton took to Twitter—specifically the new @Kensington-Royal handle—to announce Charlotte's arrival. (The royal easel was posted next.) Thanks to the Succession to the Crown Act 2013, Princess Charlotte became fourth in line to the throne. This time, Kate exited the hospital just ten hours after giving birth and chose a custom white-and-yellow floral dress, again by Jenny Packham. Prince George also famously dropped by to meet his baby sister, wearing a royal-blue jumper (the British word for sweater) that matched his dad, Prince William, and nervously waving at the crowds.

As for Prince Louis Arthur Charles of Cambridge, he arrived on April 23, 2018, at 11:01 a.m. weighing 8 pounds and 7 ounces. Kate and William—pros at the whole parenting thing at this point—left the Lindo Wing at St. Mary's Hospital just seven hours after his arrival. This time her dress—bright red with a Peter Pan collar—was said to nod to Princess Diana again, as the dress she wore to celebrate the arrival of Prince Harry outside the Lindo Wing in 1984 was also bright red. Kate and William first announced the delivery on their @Kensington-

Royal Instagram account, photos included. Prince Louis is fifth in line to the throne. Another important detail: his name is pronounced Lou-ee (not Lou-iss).

What animal did Prince George interact with on tour with his parents in Australia that caused the entire world to swoon?

*I*t was William and Kate's first royal tour with baby—and Prince George's first public appearance since his christening. In April 2014, they traveled to Australia and New Zealand for two weeks with Prince George, who was just nine months old. He quickly proved to be a total scene-stealer, upstaging his mum and dad at nearly every appearance he was able to join, specifically a trip to the Taronga Zoo in Sydney.

There, he was introduced to a real live bilby, who just so happened to be named after him. (He was originally named Boy, but he was renamed George in July 2013 in honor of the prince's birth.) George's reaction to the marsupial? Squeals of delight. He also couldn't help gripping the edge of the glass "fence" in an attempt to get a better look. On the flip side, when he was handed a stuffed bilby—a toy gifted to him by the zoo—he immediately discarded it, tossing it on the ground. (Kate cringed just a bit.)

The entire trip was a huge success with headlines touting significant (and growing) support of the monarchy.

With Princess Charlotte's arrival, which outdated royal rule did the queen decide to change?

The rule in question is called the Succession to the Crown Act 2013. The act states that the gender of a royal born after October 28, 2011, does not give that person, or their descendants, precedence over anyone else in determining the next monarch. When it was passed by Parliament, it abolished the royal requirement (which dates back to 1701) that an heir to the throne had to be male. But fun fact: Originally, the law wasn't updated to apply to Princess Charlotte. It was written to apply to Prince George, who arrived on July 22, 2013. Parliament even rushed its passing, given that Kate Middleton was expecting and, at the time, no one knew that her firstborn, George, would be a he and not a she.

Instead it was Princess Charlotte who would make history when she was born on May 2, 2015. For so many, solidifying her position as fourth in line to the throne after Prince George was a no-brainer, given that recent monarchs included both Queen Victoria (who reigned for sixty-four years) and Queen

Elizabeth II (who's nearing a mega-milestone of 70 years and counting on the throne).

Of course, Queen Elizabeth II was only named monarch after her father, King George VI, and his wife, Queen Elizabeth, didn't produce any male heirs. If they had, Princess Elizabeth never would have ascended the throne as royal sons took precedence over daughters—even those who were firstborn—in accordance with the now-outdated royal rule.

It's worth noting that the Succession to the Crown Act 2013 wasn't retroactive when passed, which meant that Princess Anne didn't suddenly jump ahead of her younger brothers Prince Andrew and Prince Edward in line to the throne.

The Cambridge family spends most of their time in London at Kensington Palace, but they also have a country home. Where is it?

William and Kate's primary residence is Apartment 1A at Kensington Palace, a four-story home with twenty rooms that's also a stone's throw from where Princess Diana used to live. (She resided in Apartments 8 and 9 before and after her divorce from Prince Charles.) It's also where Princess Margaret used to live.

But Anmer Hall, located on the royal family's Sandringham Estate in Norfolk, England, is their countryside escape. (It's also where they lived for the majority of the COVID-19 pandemic, riding out the UK's many lockdowns.) The ten-bedroom property was a gift from the queen upon their marriage in April 2011. When the Cambridges first acquired the home, they spent more than $2 million revamping the interior of the Georgian-style estate (originally constructed in 1802) as well as making updates to the grounds, which include a tennis court and swimming pool. One of the biggest changes by Kate and William was to make the kitchen the center of the home. (They're known to love to entertain.) They also added a glass-lined "garden room," according to *Town & Country* magazine.

Up until 2017, Anmer Hall was the primary address for Kate and William until they relocated to London, likely to be closer to the kids' school. Now, aside from the pandemic, Anmer Hall is a much-loved spot for the Cambridges, especially for summer vacations and Christmas. Kate in particular is known to love the low-key character of the estate. On the *Happy Mum, Happy Baby* podcast, host Giovanna Fletcher asked Kate when she's happiest. Her reply? "When I'm with my family outside in the countryside, and we're filthy dirty."

Sadly, the Cambridge family dog, given to them in 2011, passed away in 2020. What was the dog's name and connection to its successor, adopted by the family in 2020?

The Cambridges' first family dog, Lupo, was a black English cocker spaniel given to Prince William and Kate Middleton in late 2011 after being born just before Christmas of the same year. Lupo was the son of Ella, James Middleton's (Kate's brother's) English cocker spaniel. He was gifted to them by James in honor of their wedding. "Lupo" is the Italian word for "wolf" and was reportedly inspired by the Duchess of Cambridge's paternal family tree. Her great-grandmother's maiden name was Lupton. The Lupton family crest depicts three wolves.

Lupo was featured prominently in the first official portrait of Prince George shortly after his birth in 2013, as well as in a photo for Prince George's third birthday—Prince George seems about to feed the dog a scoop of ice cream at a picnic. Lupo also appeared in British *Vogue* for Kate's cover issue in June 2016.

Sadly, Lupo died in mid-November 2020 at age nine. The Cambridges posted a photo to their official Instagram account with the caption: "Very sadly last weekend our dear dog, Lupo, passed away. He has been at the heart of our family for the past nine years and we will miss him so much. – W & C."

Kate's brother James gifted William and Kate a new dog before Lupo passed: a black English cocker spaniel, niece to Lupo. (Lupo's sister, Luna, is the new puppy's mother.) While we still don't know the name, all signs point to an *L* moniker!

Kate Middleton was recently awarded the highest rank of chivalry personally granted by the sovereign. What was it?

*I*n April 2019, the Duchess of Cambridge was appointed Dame Grand Cross of the Royal Victorian Order (GCVO), the highest rank of chivalry the queen can personally bestow to recognize one's service to the sovereign. The Dame Grand Cross is the female equivalent of a knight and is a tremendous distinction, reaffirming the queen's respect and admiration for her granddaughter-in-law.

The appointment was announced on Kate's eighth wedding anniversary to Prince William. One month later, a private ceremony was held to invest the duchess with the honor.

Then, in June, at a state banquet, Kate proudly repped her Dame Grand Cross status with a royal-blue sash worn over her white ruffled lace Alexander McQueen gown. The sash is also worn with the Royal Victorian Order's badge, a white enamel Maltese cross with a Tudor crown, as well as an eight-pointed star with a smaller version of the badge in its center.

As the name implies, the award was established by Queen Victoria in 1896. The appointments are made directly by the sovereign and honor great personal service to the monarch or the monarch's family members. Other current Dames Grand Cross recipients include Princess Anne; Camilla, Duchess of Cornwall; and Sophie, Countess of Wessex.

Kate Middleton's latest passion project is the 5 Big Questions on the Under Fives. Prince William recently launched his Earthshot campaign. Why are these two endeavors of particular importance to the Cambridges?

We'll start with the Duchess of Cambridge. Since joining the royal family, her philanthropic endeavors have largely focused on family and children, especially around "the early years," defined as prebirth to five years of age. So it's no wonder her first solo project as a working royal, the 5 Big Questions Survey, has been a culmination of nearly eight years of work. It reflects a true passion for helping to improve the social, emotional, psychological, and physical well-being of children and families in the UK and around the world.

During the COVID-19 pandemic, in late 2020, Kate revealed the findings of her 5 Big Questions Survey in the form of 5 Big Insights. The survey was the largest of its kind in British history, garnering 500,000 responses about early childhood education and support among family charities. In 2021 she also announced the launch of the Royal Foundation Centre for Early Childhood, which will shine an even bigger spotlight on the impact of the first five years of life on future outcomes.

As a mother of three, Kate seems to take the cause very much to heart, but she's also made it clear that her "mum" status isn't a requirement for the championing of family causes. "Parenthood isn't a prerequisite for understanding the importance of the early years," Kate said during her 5 Big Insights forum. "If we only expect people to take an interest in the early years when they have children, we are not only too late for them, we are underestimating the huge role others can play in shaping our most formative years, too."

As for William, his biggest initiative to date is the Earthshot Prize, an annual environmental award that will amount to the doling out of £50 million over ten years. He launched the climate-conservation award along with Sir David Attenborough in 2020. It seems he's following in his father's footsteps, as Prince Charles has also focused his philanthropic work on drawing attention to climate change and sustainability.

Still, it was the Duke of Cambridge's children that he credited with his increased interest in the area. In his own documentary, *Prince William: A Planet for Us All*, William said "I've got George,

Charlotte, now Louis. Your outlook does change. And that's why I knew I had to do something."

Which celeb is kind of a big deal in the Cambridge household (and also helped inspire Prince William's recent work on climate change)?

Sure, the Cambridges have rubbed elbows with quite a few famous faces (Roger Federer, Reese Witherspoon, and Elton John to name a few). But the celeb with peak star status in their household is surprisingly the ninety-five-year-old natural historian and English broadcaster David Attenborough.

How did this come to be? Kate Middleton herself revealed in a video call with Casterton Primary Academy during the pandemic that Prince George is quite interested in Attenborough's work—specifically his documentary *Blue Planet*—so much so that it's elevated Attenborough's position as the best famous person they'd ever met (a question served up by the students, of course).

But their relationship with Attenborough is much more deep-rooted than that. The historian is in fact the same age as Queen Elizabeth II, and the pair have enjoyed a long-term friendship. Prince Charles even met him during a tour of the BBC television studios in 1958 when he was ten years old. Kate has also met the historian before, joining him for the naming ceremony of the RRS *Sir David Attenborough* while Prince William has referred to him as a "national treasure."

Speaking of Prince William, Attenborough and his impact on Prince George is said to have been one of the major reasons the future king of England set out to launch the Earthshot Prize, the biggest environmental prize ever. He's even tag teaming the initiative with Attenborough. Together, the pair celebrated its launch in fall 2020 via an Instagram Q&A with questions posed by the Cambridge kids themselves. (From Prince George: "Hello David Attenborough, what animal do you think will become extinct next?")

Kate Middleton uses emojis…just like us! The Duchess revealed some of her most-used emojis during a Q&A for her 5 Big Questions project. What were they?

*D*uring the culmination of her 5 Big Questions project in November 2020, the Duchess of Cambridge hosted a virtual Q&A about the project's findings. Commenters were asked to submit questions about the early years via comments on an @KensingtonRoyal Instagram post.

Before answering a select batch of comments, Kate thanked everyone who sent in questions, saying, "A huge number here with loads of really wonderful emojis." She then turned her phone to the camera, inadvertently showing off a slew of "most-used" emojis as the bottom of her own phone screen... and they weren't exactly what you'd expect from the Duchess (no crowns or castles here!).

They reportedly included the sliced cucumber emoji, the swearing face, the pineapple, the space invader, vomiting face, a wind gust, and two girls holding hands (though it's extremely difficult to tell from the split-second moment).

Of course, this is assuming the Duchess used her own phone for the Q&A, which is definitely not a given, considering the Cambridges' social media team could easily have swapped in one of their phones for her to use instead.

The royal family typically keeps health matters private, which is why Prince William is said to have delayed announcing he had contracted which virus in April 2020?

*A*ll right, this one's a gimme. In November 2020, news broke that Prince William had contracted COVID-19 months ago, in April. That would mean William was fighting the virus a few weeks after his father, Prince Charles, also came down with it. The reason for not spilling the news of his infection sooner? Reportedly, the Duke of Cambridge didn't want to "alarm the nation."

"There were important things going on and I didn't want to worry anyone," he reportedly told an attendee at one of his engagements in the fall, according to the *Sun*. William was well looked after during his illness, though. He self-isolated at Anmer Hall in Norfolk and was treated by palace doctors. Remarkably, Prince William also carried out Zoom and telephone engagements during his time with COVID. In late May 2021, both William and Kate shared on social media that they had received their vaccinations. (William's pic got quite the reaction, given that it showed off his biceps; Kate garnered attention for her casual dress code—mom jeans and a cap sleeve tee, although she did wear her twelve-carat engagement ring.)

Throughout the pandemic, the royal family had a few additional brushes with the virus. Although it wasn't actually revealed whether she tested positive, Sophie, Countess of Wessex, self-isolated after learning of a possible exposure to COVID. And Kate, while in attendance at the 2021 Wimbledon Championships post-vaccination, was said to have come in contact with someone who later tested positive for the virus. (Kate self-isolated as a precaution.) Finally, an ode to Captain Sir Tom Moore, who gained global recognition for walking laps in his garden and raising nearly £39 million for the NHS, was knighted by the queen in July 2020, contracted COVID-19 and passed away at age one hundred in February 2021.

Kate Middleton and Prince William recently celebrated ten years of marriage with brand-new official portraits. But they also took an influencer turn with the unveiling of what else?

On April 29, 2021, the internet was in a tizzy over the release of not one, but two brand-new anniversary portraits from the Duke and Duchess of Cambridge. But this wasn't just any anniversary—Kate and William were celebrating ten years of marriage, not just with a couple of new snaps (both shot by UK-based photographer Chris Floyd), but also with a thirty-nine-second video that showcased their family life, George, Charlotte, and Louis all included.

About the portraits: shot at Kensington Palace, Kate and William appeared unusually touchy-feely, holding hands in one of the images, while another appears to be a recreation of their engagement portrait, shot a decade earlier by Mario Testino.

Still, it was the video—beautifully composed by filmmaker Will Warr—that caused the world's heart to flutter: Kate and William are shown frolicking with their kids on a Norfolk beach, assumed to be located not far from their country home,

Anmer Hall. They're also shown roasting marshmallows, chasing after the kids on a grassy field, and climbing a tree. There's even a shot of Princess Charlotte and Prince Louis on a seesaw together. Accompanying the clip was a message, signed by W & C: "Thank you to everyone for the kind messages on our wedding anniversary. We are enormously grateful for the 10 years of support we have received in our lives as a family."

The Cambridges as influencers? Perhaps. On the heels of their portrait release and video launch, they also rebranded their Instagram handle from @KensingtonRoyal to @DukeandDuchessofCambridge. In addition to that, they officially announced their own YouTube channel, splitting off from the royal family's YouTube presence to carve out a space that's all their own.

It was considered to be one of the most anticipated royal events of the year: the unveiling of the Princess Diana statue. But an additional layer of drama overshadowed the occasion. What was it?

*I*n July 2021, Princes William and Harry reunited for a long-anticipated reunion in London and in the very spot their mother Princess Diana used to feel most at home: the Sunken Garden at Kensington Palace. The occasion? To unveil the Princess Diana statue they'd commissioned sculptor Ian

Rank-Broadley to create in 2017 to honor Diana in her 60th birthday year. (The statement they issued at the time said, "It has been twenty years since our mother's death and the time is right to recognize her positive impact in the UK and around the world with a permanent statue. Our mother touched so many lives.")

But since that announcement, a lot had happened: Prince Harry and Meghan Markle had married, then shared their decision to quit their roles as senior members of the royal family. The pair moved to Canada, then California. The COVID-19 pandemic hit, and details of a much deeper family rift began to play out. (See Part II, "The Sussexes," for more on everything that went down.) Other than reuniting briefly to say goodbye to their grandfather Prince Philip in April 2021, the statue unveiling was the first time William and Harry would be pictured together at a formal royal engagement, and an intimate one at that.

Just a handful of people (Diana's siblings included) were present for the unveiling of the bronze statue and, while brief, it went off without a hitch. (Prince Charles, Kate Middleton, and Meghan Markle weren't present at the occasion.) The brothers were cordial toward each other, despite rumors that they're barely on speaking terms, and smiled and appeared to joke around a bit, too. They also released another joint statement: "Today, on what would have been our Mother's 60th birthday, we remember her love, strength and character—qualities that made her a force for good around the world, changing countless lives for the better. Every day, we wish she were still with us, and our hope is that this statue will be seen forever as a symbol of her life and her legacy."

PART II

THE SUSSEXES

Just like Prince William, Prince Harry was born at St. Mary's Hospital in London. But his real name isn't Harry. What is it?

Sound the royal bugles: Prince Harry's official name is actually Prince Henry. Henry Charles Albert David Mountbatten-Windsor was born to a twenty-three-year-old Princess Diana on Saturday, September 15, 1984, at 4:20 p.m. in the famous Lindo Wing of St. Mary's Hospital—where Kate Middleton, his sister-in-law, would go on to deliver her three children three decades later. Harry—or Henry, if you want to get technical—weighed 6 pounds, 14 ounces, and followed his two-year-old brother William in the line of succession.

A TV crewman waiting outside the hospital first broke the news of the baby's birth after Diana's nine-hour labor. "It's a boy!" he shouted to the crowds of reporters and well-wishers. "We've nearly got a full polo team now," Prince Charles, thirty-five, later told the throngs standing outside the hospital. He also told the crowd, "I'm going to go home and have a stiff drink."

Buckingham Palace's statement announcing the name of Charles and Diana's second son was released less than twenty-four hours after his birth and clarified that the baby would officially go by his full name, Prince Henry Charles Albert David, but would be known just as "Harry" to his friends and family.

The media initially reported that Diana and Charles had hoped for a girl. Although the betting odds heavily favored the first name "George" if the baby were a boy (it was said Charles wanted to honor his grandfather, King George VI), "Henry" was an outside contender with 50:1 odds. In *Diana: Her True Story*, written by Andrew Morton, Princess Diana revealed Prince Charles wanted to name their sons Albert and Arthur, but Diana felt the names were too outdated. "No, too old!" she said on one of the tapes, and chose William and Harry instead.

Prince Harry's wife, Meghan Markle, also was born with a different name than what she currently goes by. What is her actual first name?

*R*achel Zane (Meghan's character on *Suits*) isn't that far of a stretch... Rachel Meghan Markle was born on August 4, 1981, in Canoga Park, Los Angeles, California, to Doria Ragland and Thomas W. Markle. She attended the private Hollywood Little Red Schoolhouse before attending the all-girls Immaculate Heart Catholic school in LA.

Meghan reflected on the early years of her life for an essay in *Elle* in 2015: "It was the late seventies when my parents met, my dad was a lighting director for a soap opera and my mom was a temp at the studio. I like to think he was drawn to her sweet eyes and her Afro, plus their shared love of antiques. Whatever it was, they married and had me. They moved into a house in the Valley in LA, to a neighbourhood that was leafy and affordable. What it was not, however, was diverse. And there was my mom, caramel in complexion with her light-skinned baby in tow, being asked where my mother was since they assumed she was the nanny."

Contrary to reports that Meghan chose the double-M alliteration to be more appealing to casting directors when trying to make it as an actress in Hollywood, she has been referred to as "Meghan" since she was a child.

In 1993, Meghan appeared on *Nick News* to bring attention to sexism she had witnessed in TV commercials. At age eleven, she had written a letter to Procter & Gamble requesting the company change their Ivory soap commercial slogan to be more inclusive. Her letter appears in the segment, with her beautiful cursive signature (yes, even at age eleven her calligraphy was top-notch) clearly reading "Meghan Markle."

Upon his birth in 1984, Prince Harry became third in line to the throne. What is his current position in the line of succession?

*P*rince Harry is currently sixth in line to the throne, after dropping down three spots in the order of succession following the birth of his nephews and niece. Currently, Prince Charles is first in line, then Prince William, then William and Kate's children (George, Charlotte, Louis), followed by Prince Harry.

Prince Harry was born third in line to the throne, but had Prince William been a girl, Harry would've been second. The same would've been true for his niece, Princess Charlotte, who could've been superseded by her younger brother Prince Louis. Thankfully, two years prior to Charlotte's birth, Queen Elizabeth changed that by passing the Succession to the Crown Act of 2013. (See Part I, "The Cambridges," for more info, but, basically, the act states that the gender of a royal born after October 28, 2011, does not give that person precedence or their descendants precedence when it comes to the line of succession.)

Prince Harry's life was changed forever upon the death of his mother, Princess Diana, in 1997. What is his biggest regret from her funeral?

*I*t was a sight few will ever forget: Prince Harry, twelve, and Prince William, fifteen, walking behind their mother's coffin during her funeral procession. While shouldering the unbearable loss of their mother's death, they followed behind Diana's cortege alongside Prince Philip; Diana's brother, Charles, 9th Earl Spencer; and Prince Charles.

Princess Diana's funeral was held on September 6, 1997, six days after the deadly Paris car crash that killed her, Dodi Al Fayed, and the driver. The funeral took place at Westminster Abbey before she was laid to rest in a private ceremony at her ancestral home of Althorp. Over 2.5 billion people around the world watched the boys solemnly following their mother's coffin—on top of which was a handwritten note from Harry, addressed to "mummy," in addition to three white wreaths and a pall featuring the royal standard—along the nearly two-mile route. Prince William said he used his longer hair and bangs as a "safety blanket" to cover his grief during the "very long, lonely walk. I felt if I looked at the floor and my hair came down over my face, no one could see me," he said during a BBC documentary for the twentieth anniversary of Diana's death.

Harry spoke about walking behind his mother's coffin in an interview with *Newsweek* in 2017. He said, "My mother had just died, and I had to walk a long way behind her coffin, surrounded by thousands of people watching me while millions more did on television. I don't think any child should be asked to do that, under any circumstances. I don't think it would happen today."

He also reflected on the moment in the first episode of Apple TV+'s *The Me You Can't See* documentary. "For me the thing I remember the most was the sound of the horses' hooves going along the Mall," Harry told his series cohost Oprah. "It was like I was outside of my body and just walking along doing what was expected of me. [I was] showing one-tenth of the emotion that everybody else was showing: This was my mum—you never even met her."

The long-term effect of losing his mother at the age of twelve caused Harry to have severe panic attacks as an adult, the prince told Oprah. "I was just all over the place mentally," he said, "Every time I put a suit on and tie on...having to do the role, and go, 'right, game face,' look in the mirror and say, 'let's go'. Before I even left the house I was pouring with sweat. I was in fight or flight mode. I was willing to drink, I was willing to take drugs, I was willing to try and do the things that made me feel less like I was feeling." He said he would drink a week's worth of alcohol on a Friday or Saturday night "not because I was enjoying it, but because I was trying to mask something."

The Duke of Sussex has also spoken about the last interaction he had with his mum: a phone conversation that was a regular occurrence after his parents' split. "I can't really, necessarily, remember what I said," Harry explained in the HBO documentary *Diana, Our Mother: Her Life and Legacy*. "But all I do remember is probably, you know, regretting for the rest of my life how short the phone call was. And if I'd known that was the last time I was going to speak to my mother—the things I would have said to her."

Before he joined the military, Prince Harry followed a similar educational path to his brother, Prince William. What schools did he attend?

$\mathcal{L}$ike his big brother, Prince Harry started his education at Jane Mynors' Nursery School in London, before attending pre-preparatory Wetherby School starting at age five. At age eight, he began attending the all-boys boarding school Ludgrove, in Berkshire, just as William had. After passing entrance exams, he was admitted to Eton College, just like William, and attended from 1998–2003.

While the decision to attend Eton went against what Harry's grandfather, father, and two uncles had done—attend Gordonstoun—it did follow his mother's family's tradition, as both Diana's father and brother had attended Eton. But Harry said he wished he had been more appreciative of the roughly $55,000/ year private school. Speaking to Nobel Prize–winning educational activist Malala Yousafzai in 2020, he said "I'm hugely grateful for the education I was lucky enough to have. At the time I certainly probably wasn't as grateful, but looking back at it now, I'm very, very blessed with having such an amazing opportunity," he added.

At age eighteen, in June 2003, Harry completed his education at Eton (though his grades were less than stellar), and secured his place at Royal Military Academy Sandhurst. Before attending the academy in 2005, though, he took a gap year in Australia, working on a cattle station like his father Prince Charles had done at that age. He also traveled to Lesotho, Africa, where he worked with orphaned children and helped produce the documentary film *The Forgotten Kingdom: Prince Harry in Lesotho*.

Prince Harry eventually found his footing as a member of the military for nearly ten years. Where was he deployed for active duty?

"*C*aptain Wales," as he was known in the military, undertook two tours of Afghanistan in 2007–2008 and 2012–2013. Harry joined the Royal Military Academy Sandhurst in 2005 and completed his British Army officer training in 2006 at age twenty-one. The following year, it was announced that Harry's regiment would be deployed to Iraq. However, after several threats from groups viewing Harry as a high-value target, it was decided he wouldn't be deployed.

Then, in February 2008, news broke: Harry had been stationed in Afghanistan for ten weeks as a forward air controller. The secret had been kept through a media blackout: the British press had agreed not to report on his whereabouts, until the *Drudge Report*, Australian magazine *New Idea* or German newspaper *Bild* (or all three, accounts vary) breached the blackout and reported that the prince was stationed overseas. Harry was brought back to the UK for his safety and the safety of his company. This made Harry the first royal to serve in an active war zone since his uncle, Prince Andrew, who flew helicopters during the Falklands War in 1982.

In September 2012, Harry began his second overseas tour of Afghanistan, this time as copilot and gunner of an Apache helicopter. Harry returned from a twenty-week deployment in January 2013, and successfully qualified as an Apache aircraft commander in July 2013.

Meghan Markle grew up in California, hanging out on TV sets, such as *Married with Children*, thanks to her father Thomas Markle. But she was also a young feminist who found her voice after a particular commercial felt offensive. What was it?

*M*eghan was an activist from the very start. One of her most well-known campaigns to bring about social change came at age eleven, when she requested Procter & Gamble change their Ivory Soap commercial slogan from "women are fighting greasy pots and pans" to "people are fighting greasy pots and pans." She also wrote to Hillary Clinton, lawyer Gloria Allred, and journalist Linda Ellerbee in addition to the president of Procter & Gamble.

About a month later, the company changed the commercial. The next year, in 1993, *Nick News* featured Meghan's story and highlighted her commitment to eradicate sexism in TV commercials at such a young age. "It's always, 'mom does this,' and 'mom does that,'" a twelve-year-old Meghan told *Nick News* host Linda Ellerbee. "If you see something you don't like on television or any other place, write letters and send them to the right people, and you can really make a difference, not just for yourself but for lots of people."

But that wasn't her first attempt to bring about social change. At age ten, Meghan organized a protest against the Gulf War when she heard one of her classmates express his anguish over his older brother leaving to fight in the war. She and her classmates held hand-drawn signs, with Meghan's reading "Peace and harmony for the world." The group was filmed by a local TV news station.

And while she didn't publicly reflect on it till years later, Meghan's parents set an example that "what is" was not necessarily "what should be," like when her father bought two Barbie doll sets for his daughter for Christmas and combined them into one mixed-race family. "When I was about seven, I had been fawning over a boxed set of Barbie dolls," Meghan wrote in an essay for *Elle* in 2015. "It was called The Heart Family and included a mom doll, a dad doll, and two children. This perfect nuclear family was only sold in sets of white dolls or black dolls. I don't remember coveting one over the other, I just wanted one. On Christmas morning, swathed in glitter-flecked wrapping paper, there I found my Heart Family: a black mom doll, a white dad doll, and a child in each colour. My dad had taken the sets apart and customised my family."

Before she was a duchess, Meghan Markle was an actress, most widely known for her leading role on the network legal drama *Suits*. What were some of her other famous acting roles?

*B*efore starring as paralegal-turned-big-shot-lawyer Rachel Zane on *Suits*, Meghan appeared on an episode of *General Hospital*, as "Briefcase model #24" on *Deal or No Deal* for two years (from 2006–2007), in two episodes of *90210*, and in crime dramas *Fringe*, *CSI: Miami*, *Without a Trace*, and *Castle*.

She also had a small part in *A Lot Like Love*, where she played the "hot girl" sitting in the seat next to Ashton Kutcher's character on an airplane. She starred as a minor character in a few other movies—*Remember Me, Get Him to the Greek, The Candidate,* and *Horrible Bosses*—before getting big movie roles in *Random Encounters* in 2013 and *Anti-Social* in 2015.

She also starred in two Hallmark movies: *When Sparks Fly* (2014) and *Dater's Handbook* (2016). But her biggest acting break came with *Suits*, which she starred in for seven seasons, from 2011 to 2018. While we'll never know what could've been had she continued acting, Meghan's publicist from 2014 to 2016, Elizabeth Tuke, told *Vanity Fair* in 2021 that she encouraged her to go after blockbusters. "You could be the next Megan Fox," Tuke told her at the time.

In addition to acting, Meghan Markle also was the creator of her very own lifestyle blog, called *The Tig*. What was the inspiration for the name of her website?

R.I.P. ***The Tig***. Meghan Markle's lifestyle blog, "a hub for the discerning palate—those with a hunger for food, travel, fashion & beauty" began in May 2014. She named the site after one of her favorite wines, Tignanello (teen-ya-nel-low), after having her first "Tig moment," an "aha moment" that she had while sipping the Italian wine.

"It wasn't just red or white," Meghan wrote. "Suddenly, I understood what people meant by the body, legs, structure of wine. It was an aha moment at its finest. For me, it became a Tig moment—a moment of getting it. From that point on, any new awareness, any new discovery or 'Ohhhhh, I get it!' moment was a Tig moment."

In a letter posted to the blog in April 2017, Meghan wrote, "After close to three beautiful years on this adventure with you, it's time to say goodbye to ***The Tig***. What began as a passion project (my little engine that could) evolved into an amazing community of inspiration, support, fun and frivolity. You've made my days brighter and filled this experience with so much joy. Keep finding those Tig moments of discovery, keep laughing and taking risks, and keep being 'the change you wish to see in the world.' Above all, don't ever forget your worth—as I've told you time and time again: you, my sweet friend, you are enough. Thank you for everything. Xx, Meghan Markle."

What long-term impact did Princess Diana's death have on Prince Harry, and what charitable organization did he dedicate to her memory?

*P*rince Harry has been candid about his struggles following the death of his mother and how they've had a profound impact on his life. Speaking to ITV's Tom Bradby during the Sussexes' Africa tour, Harry said his mother's death is "a wound that festers."

"I think being part of this family, in this role, in this job, every single time I see a camera, every single time I hear a click, every single time I see a flash, it takes me straight back," he said. "So, in that respect, it's the worst reminder of her life, as opposed to the best."

Prince Harry's charity, Sentebale, which means "forget me not," was founded in his mother's honor. The organization helps vulnerable and orphaned children in Lesotho, Africa, many of whom are living with HIV/AIDS. Sentebale cofounder Prince Seeiso of Lesotho also lost his mother. "I wanted to do something to make my mother proud," Harry said in the 2016 documentary, *Prince Harry in Africa.*

And in March 2021, the duke penned a foreword to a children's book called *Hospital on the Hill* to help kids deal with the loss of a loved one to COVID. "When I was a young boy, I lost my mum," he wrote. "At the time I didn't want to believe it or accept it, and it left a huge hole inside of me," Prince Harry wrote. "I know how you feel, and I want to assure you that over time that hole will be filled with so much love and support."

"We all cope with loss in a different way, but when a parent goes to heaven, I was told their spirit, their love and the memories of them do not," he continued. "They are always with you, and you can hold on to them forever. I find this to be true."

But Harry wasn't always this open about his mum's tragic accident. In 2016, the prince told reporters, "I really regret not ever talking about it. For the first twenty-eight years of my life, I never talked about it."

Prince Harry and Meghan Markle famously debuted their relationship in Toronto at an event honoring an organization that is near and dear to Harry's heart. What is it?

At the 2017 Invictus Games, Meghan and Harry stepped out as an official couple. Holding hands as they arrived and smiling as they sat together to watch the opening ceremony in Toronto, Meghan and Harry looked smitten and relaxed. She wore a white button-down called the "Husband Shirt" by Misha Nonoo (a foreshadowing of events to come) and distressed jeans by Mother. And a true sign of a relationship getting serious? Meghan's mother, Doria Ragland, joined the couple for the games' closing ceremony to spend time with her daughter's new beau (and soon-to-be fiancé).

Prince Harry founded the Invictus Games, an international competition for wounded and injured servicemen and servicewomen, in 2014. His goal in founding the organization was to harness the power of sport and competition to inspire recovery, support rehabilitation, and generate a wider understanding and respect of all those serving in the military.

The Sussexes' first confirmed production with Netflix will center on the stories of competitors of the Invictus Games that will take place in The Hague in 2022. Titled *Heart of Invictus*, the show will "reveal powerful stories of resilience and hope."

Their courtship was a whirlwind, but Prince Harry famously described to James Corden that royal dating is different... and easy to expedite. How come?

*R*oyal dating is all backwards, according to Prince Harry. "Dating with me, or with any member of the royal family I guess, is kind of flipped upside down," Harry told Corden during his appearance on *The Late Late Show* in early 2021. "All the dates become dinners or watching the TV or chatting at home. And then eventually, once you become a couple, you venture out to dinners, to the cinema, and everything else. So, everything was done back to front with us. So actually we got to spend an enormous amount of time just the two of us, rather than going to friends' houses or out to dinner where there are other distractions... We went from zero to sixty in the first two months," Harry revealed.

Those first two months started in July 2016 when the pair were set up on a blind date through a mutual friend. Reportedly, the couple dined at Soho House's Dean Street Townhouse in London. Harry also told Corden, "The second date, I was starting to think 'wow, this is pretty special.'" During those first few months, the couple reportedly texted every day, and Meghan even followed Prince Harry's private Instagram account. Then, for their third date, Prince Harry swept Meghan off her feet for a surprise five-day trip to Botswana, where the couple "camped out with each other under the stars, sharing a tent and all that stuff. It was fantastic," Harry said during their engagement interview.

In November 2016, Kensington Palace released a statement confirming their relationship and slamming the racist and sexist treatment of Meghan in the press. In April 2017, Meghan shut down *The Tig*. Then, in September, Meghan and Harry made their couple debut at the Invictus Games in Toronto. In November 2017, the pair announced their engagement with a romantic photo shoot in the Sunken Garden of Kensington Palace, supposedly one of Princess Diana's favorite places when she lived at the palace.

What wedding did Meghan Markle sneak into in an effort to keep their relationship hush-hush?

*M*eghan Markle: wedding crasher? Not quite. Reportedly, Harry snuck then-girlfriend Meghan into Pippa Middleton and James Matthews's wedding in May 2017 so as not to draw undue attention from the press (plus, Pippa and James reportedly had a "no ring, no bring" policy for guests). While most of the media said Harry took a three-hour, one-hundred-mile round trip to pick up Markle and bring her to the reception after attending the ceremony solo, it's more likely Meghan had already made the trip to Berkshire with Harry that morning, then waited at nearby Englefield House till after the ceremony so she could join him for the evening festivities.

Yep, in the first year of their relationship, Harry and Meghan were trying to stay out of the spotlight as much as possible, though Meghan did confirm her relationship with Harry in September 2017 in the October issue of *Vanity Fair*. "We're a couple. We're in love. I'm sure there will be a time when we will have to come forward and present ourselves and have stories to tell, but I hope what people will understand is that this is our time. This is for us. It's part of what makes it so special, that it's just ours. But we're happy," Meghan told the magazine.

According to their engagement interview, Prince Harry proposed over roast chicken. But with what ring?

*J*n August 2017, Prince Harry popped the question to Meghan Markle. It had been almost exactly a year since the couple's third date, a trip to Botswana in 2016 (according to *Finding Freedom* by royal biographers Omid Scobie and

Carolyn Durand). The prince proposed with a three-stone ring set in gold that he designed himself with the help of royal jeweler Cleave & Company. The center stone is a cushion-cut diamond from Botswana—thought to be a romantic callout to their first trip there—estimated to be about three carats, while the two round side stones are from Princess Diana's collection and are estimated at about 1.5 carats each.

According to the couple, Harry could barely get the question out before Meghan said "Yes!" During the TV interview the couple gave immediately after announcing their engagement in November 2017, Harry recalled that it was "a standard, typical night for us" at Nottingham Cottage in Kensington Palace. "It was a cozy night...what were we doing? Trying to roast a chicken," Meghan added, recalling that Harry got down on one knee. "As a matter of fact, I could barely let you finish proposing," Meghan said, imitating her own eagerness. "'Can I say yes now?!'"

Meghan's ring was paired with a wedding band of Welsh gold on the couple's wedding day, and has gone through at least one change since Prince Harry proposed to her with it in 2017. After she announced her pregnancy, it was noted that Meghan appeared in public a few times without her engagement ring. Then, with its presence on her finger at Trooping the Colour in 2019, news outlets picked up that the ring had undergone a transformation: the addition of pavé stones on the band.

Just as with Kate Middleton and Princess Diana, speculation over Meghan Markle's wedding dress designer was at an all-time high leading up to the wedding date. Who designed her dress?

*A*nd the winner is...Clare Waight Keller for Givenchy. Only six months into her role as artistic director when she was selected to create Meghan's dress, the British-born designer was also the first female creative lead of the French fashion house. The dress unveiling came as Meghan exited the car with her mom in front of the steps of St. George's Chapel. Understated and minimalist, the simplicity drew attention to the dress's exquisite details.

Kensington Palace released a statement immediately after the big reveal. It read: "The dress epitomizes a timeless minimal elegance referencing the codes of the iconic House of Givenchy and showcasing the expert craftsmanship of its world-renowned Parisian couture atelier founded in 1952. True to the heritage of the house, the pure lines of the dress are achieved using six meticulously placed seams. The focus of the dress is the graphic open bateau neckline that gracefully frames the shoulders and emphasizes the slender sculpted waist. The lines of the dress extend towards the back where the train flows in soft round folds cushioned by an underskirt in triple silk organza. The slim three-quarter sleeves add a note of refined modernity."

The veil was sixteen-and-a-half feet long and made of silk tulle. It featured embroidery of fifty-three flowers representative of each of the Commonwealth nations. It also included wintersweet, a bloom that grows outside of Nottingham Cottage at Kensington Palace, and the California poppy, to represent the bride and groom.

On her Instagram, Keller later recalled, "Purity and simplicity were the guiding principles, a narrative of nature through the 53 florals of the Commonwealth to bring the world into the journey of the ceremony." She also wanted to "capture the classical timeless beauty I knew [Meghan] wanted to achieve. It was obvious the significance of this occasion was more than any other, it would be a very personal ceremony with so many choices that would reflect both the bride and groom's heritage and their unique way of being incredibly inclusive, genuine and generous."

And Meghan Markle's "something blue" was a special callout to her first date with Prince Harry. What was it?

The Duchess of Sussex revealed that her "something blue" was a scrap of fabric from the dress she wore on her first date with Prince Harry, reportedly at Soho House's Dean Street Townhouse in July 2016.

During the 2018 HBO documentary *Queen of the World*, Meghan talks about her wedding while looking at the dress on display, the first time she had seen it since her wedding day. "Somewhere in here, there's a piece... Did you see it? The piece of blue fabric that's stitched inside? It's fabric from my dress that I wore on our first date," Meghan told the interviewer.

While we aren't sure what her blue dress looked like, Meghan definitely swept Harry off his feet. During their engagement interview in November 2017, Meghan revealed that the first meeting "was a blind date," and they were set up by a mutual friend, who wanted "to protect her privacy." Prince Harry said, "I was beautifully surprised when I walked into that room and saw her. I was like, 'Okay, well I'm going to have to up my game.'"

And that's not the only "something blue" Meghan included in her wedding day. After an outfit change from her Givenchy wedding dress to a Stella McCartney silk-crepe white high-neck gown (and Harry to a black tux), the newlyweds hopped into an ice-blue vintage Jaguar E-type Concept Zero (manufactured in 1968 but converted to an electric model). Meghan wore her late mother-in-law's emerald-cut aquamarine cocktail ring—thought to be a gift from Prince Harry and last worn by

Princess Diana at the pre-party for the Christie's auction of Diana's wardrobe in 1997.

A wedding fit for a prince and his American princess was, of course, one of the hottest tickets of the year (if not the decade). What celebrity and famous friend of the couple not only attended, but DJ'd at the reception?

*L*adies and gents (and majesties), put your hands together for: DJ Idris Elba! That's right, the *Avengers: Infinity War* and *Concrete Cowboy* actor spun the tracks for Meghan and Harry's nighttime reception. Speaking to Ellen DeGeneres, Elba revealed how the initial ask came about: "So Harry and I have hung out a couple of times through his dad's charity—the Prince's Trust—which helped me out when I was a young actor. Harry came to a couple of parties that I DJ'd, and he was like, 'What are you doing on [May 19]?'" Elba continued, "I told him nothing and then he asked if I would DJ at his wedding... I was like, is this a joke?"

Nope, not a joke. Elba also revealed to BBC Radio 1Xtra that Meghan gave him a playlist of some of her favorite songs, and that he played "I Wanna Dance with Somebody" by Whitney Houston for the couple. When the interviewer pressed him for more info, Elba admitted that Meghan paid tribute to her California roots. "There was some West Coast [on the playlist]," Elba said. "That's all I'm saying! I'm not gonna put their business out like that."

But his audience was relatively small (compared to the six-hundred-person ceremony). The couple whittled down their guest list to two hundred for their private nighttime reception at Windsor's Frogmore House. While the party was super exclusive (with confirmed details few and far between), we do know that A-listers like George and Amal Clooney, Serena Williams and Alexis Ohanian, Priyanka Chopra Jonas, and Oprah were all at St. George's Chapel to witness the couple's vows (along with two of Harry's exes: Cressida Bonas and Chelsy Davy).

Another celebrity performed at the lunchtime reception. Kensington Palace confirmed Elton John, who was a friend of Princess Diana's and performed at her funeral, set the musical tone for their daytime event. "Prince Harry asked Sir Elton to perform at the reception, which was hosted by Her Majesty The Queen at St George's Hall, Windsor Castle," the statement read. "Sir Elton performed for the newly married couple in recognition of the close connection he has with Prince Harry and his family."

Details from *Finding Freedom*, the Sussex biography by Omid Scobie and Carolyn Durand, shed a little more light on the cellphone-less nighttime reception: hand-drawn invites for their two hundred guests, tables named for foods with different British and American pronunciations ("tomato," "oregano," and "basil"), a speech by the bride, a locally sourced all-organic menu chosen by Prince Charles, James Corden in a Henry VIII costume, and fireworks. Oh, and the couple's first dance? The 1968 hit "I'm in Love" by Wilson Pickett. But the rumor that George Clooney was handing out shots of Casamigos tequila to reception attendees? Hey, we can dream...

Prince Harry broke with tradition on his wedding day by what he wore. What was it?

*H*onorable mention to his frock coat Blues and Royals uniform. The answer we were looking for, though, was a wedding ring. Unlike his grandfather and brother, Harry opted for a wedding band that he's worn ever since his wedding day. Both his and Meghan's rings were fashioned by court jewelers Cleave & Company.

The Duke of Sussex's ring also breaks from tradition in style: It's made of platinum instead of the traditional Welsh gold that's gifted by the queen from the now inoperative Welsh mine Clogau St. David's. (Royals have had their wedding rings made from the Welsh gold since 1923.) Harry's band is also unique in that it has a slightly brushed, textured finish.

His father, Prince Charles, does have a wedding ring, but instead of the traditional ring finger, Prince Charles wears it on his pinky, next to his signet ring. (Prince William prefers not to wear a wedding ring at all.)

Meghan Markle and Prince Harry recently revealed they actually got married before the worldwide event at St. George's Chapel that was watched by over twenty-nine million in the U.S. alone. When was this other wedding date and who was in attendance?

During their bombshell sit-down interview with Oprah Winfrey in March 2021, Meghan and Harry revealed they actually married May 16, days before their royal wedding. "I was thinking about it, you know our wedding—three days before our wedding, we got married," Meghan revealed. "No one knows that. We called the archbishop, and we just said, look, this thing, this spectacle is for the world. But we want our union between us, so the vows that we have framed in our room are just the two of us in our backyard with the Archbishop of Canterbury."

The British tabloids had a field day, pointing to their legal marriage certificate that lists a wedding date of May 19 as proof the couple was lying. However, a spokesperson for the Sussexes clarified that the couple "privately exchanged personal vows a few days before their official/legal wedding on May 19." Archbishop Justin Welby backed this up in an interview with Italian newspaper *la Repubblica* by revealing that he did meet with the couple multiple times before their wedding on May 19, but that he couldn't disclose what happened at those meetings.

"If any of you ever talk to a priest, you expect them to keep that talk confidential. It doesn't matter who I'm talking to," Welby said. "I had a number of private and pastoral meetings with the duke and duchess before the wedding. The legal wedding was on the Saturday. I signed the wedding certificate, which is a legal document, and I would have committed a serious criminal offense if I signed it knowing it was false. So you can make what you like about it. But the legal wedding was on the Saturday. But I won't say what happened at any other meetings."

We guess when your grandmother is the queen, your wedding gifts are pretty impressive. What nineteenth-century mansion did Her Majesty bestow on the newly married royal couple?

Whether or not Meghan and Harry registered at Williams-Sonoma, we know one gift took the (wedding) cake: Frogmore Cottage. A gift from Her Majesty the Queen, Frogmore Cottage was Meghan and Harry's second UK residence after vacating Nottingham Cottage at Kensington Palace just a few weeks before baby Archie's arrival in 2019.

The nineteenth-century Grade II historic cottage is situated on the grounds of Windsor Castle. Rumors of major renovations (a yoga studio with a "floating" springboard floor, soundproofing, and a gym) caused quite a stir among the British tabloids, though reports of a yoga studio and other furnishings were found to be false. It was later confirmed via the Sovereign Grant that structural renovations—like updating the electrical and heating systems to current environmental standards and converting the five "dormitory-style units" into a single family home—totaled $3 million in public funds, but that the Sussexes paid for all the interior furnishings themselves. In 2020, following their official departure as senior members of the royal family, Harry and Meghan revealed that they had paid back all Frogmore renovation costs.

After the Sussexes relocated to California in 2020, the newly renovated cottage got new residents: Princess Eugenie and Jack Brooksbank, who welcomed their first child, August Philip Hawke Brooksbank, in February 2021. However, the Sussexes have stated that when they are in the UK, they still plan to use Frogmore as their home base. (Their lump-sum repayment also reportedly covered future rent on the property for an undisclosed period of time.)

Meghan Markle and Prince Harry completed two overseas royal tours before stepping down as senior royals. Where did they go?

First stop: Australia, New Zealand, Fiji, and Tonga. The Sussexes' trip to Oceania was their first royal tour as a married couple and took place in October 2018. The sixteen-day tour kicked off with a huge announcement: Meghan was pregnant! The Duke and Duchess of Sussex announced their happy news the day their trip began.

While in Oceania, the couple focused on conservation, environmental sustainability efforts, and youth leadership. A major highlight for the pair while visiting the four Commonwealth countries: attending the 2018 Invictus Games in Sydney.

Next up: the Sussexes' royal tour of Africa in the fall of 2019. They brought along then five-month-old Archie, making him one of the youngest royals to ever go on tour. (Prince George also went on a royal tour when he was a baby, at just nine months old.) The family of three began their visit in South Africa, then Prince Harry visited Malawi, Botswana, and Angola solo. While there, the Sussexes championed wildlife conservation and counter-poaching efforts, socioeconomic challenges facing young people, female empowerment, as well as making a few important stops that nodded to Princess Diana's humanitarian work in the country. (Most notably, Harry put on the same body armor and protective visor Diana had worn in 1997 to walk through a partially cleared minefield in Dirico, Angola, then visited the same site his mother walked in Huambo, which is now a thriving community.)

During their ten-day tour, they also were interviewed for a documentary by ITV, called *Harry & Meghan: An African Journey*, where they both spoke to friend and journalist Tom Bradby about struggles they faced in the past year. For Harry, the intense media attention reminded him of his mother, and he also opened up about his sibling dynamic with Prince William at a time when rumors of a rift were beginning to bubble up: "Part of this role and part of this job, this family, being under the pressure that it's under, inevitably stuff happens," Harry said. "But look, we're brothers, we'll always be brothers. We're certainly on different paths at the moment, but I'll always be there for him and as I know he'll always be there for me."

Meghan said she struggled with motherhood while under intense media scrutiny: "Look, any woman, especially when they're pregnant, you're really vulnerable, and so that was made really challenging, and then when you have a newborn... And especially as a woman, it's really, it's a lot. So, you add this on top of just trying to be a new mom or trying to be a newlywed... And also thank you for asking, because not many people have asked if I'm okay, but it's a very real thing to be going through behind the scenes." "As in it's really been a struggle?" Bradby asked. "Yes," Meghan responded.

Many of the details surrounding the birth of Prince Harry and Meghan Markle's first child were kept private, but we do know when and where baby Archie was born. What hospital was he delivered in?

On May 6, 2019, at 5:26 a.m., Meghan and Harry welcomed baby Archie into the world. His birth certificate revealed that he was born at the Portland Hospital in London and weighed 7 pounds, 3 ounces. The swanky, private, maternity-only hospital near Regent's Park is also where Princesses Beatrice and Eugenie were born, as well as Eugenie's son (and Archie's second cousin), August Brooksbank. The Sussexes' Archewell announcement—released a year later—noted that the Greek word *arche*, meaning "source of action," served as the inspiration for Archie's name.

Proud first-time dad Harry opted to hold a mini press conference in front of the horse stables at Windsor Castle instead of the typical Lindo Wing-esque reveal. "It's been the most amazing experience I could ever have possibly imagined," a beaming Harry told reporters on May 6, 2019. "How any woman does what they do is beyond comprehension, but we're both absolutely thrilled and so grateful for all the love and support from everybody out there. It's been amazing, so I just wanted to share this with everybody."

"As every father and parent would ever say, your baby is absolutely amazing," he continued. "This little thing is absolutely to die for. So I'm just over the moon." At the end, after thanking the camera crew and reporters, the flustered prince even gave a quick "thank you" to the horses in the stables behind him— which seems totally acceptable, considering he'd probably pulled an all-nighter.

Other details surrounding his birth, like the identity of Archie's godparents, were kept private. We do know he was christened in the private chapel at Windsor Castle on July 6, 2019, by the Archbishop of Canterbury. While the christening service itself is always private, unlike the christenings of Prince William and Kate Middleton's three children, reporters and press were not allowed to be present for arrivals of the royal family to the church. This, coupled with the decision to break from royal tradition and not release the names of Archie's godparents, sent the tabloids into a tizzy.

From the two photos that were released from the event, as well as other reports, we do know that about twenty-five people attended the christening, including the Cambridges; Charles and Camilla; Meghan's mother, Doria Ragland; Princess Diana's sisters, Lady Jane and Lady Sarah; and the godparents. Archie was christened in the same Honiton lace christening gown that his cousins, George, Charlotte, and Louis, were also christened in.

It was meant to be the dawn of Sussex Royal, the brand. But instead, the news of Prince Harry and Meghan Markle's decision to step down as senior royals in January 2020 took a different turn. How come?

After what was widely considered an extremely successful tour of southern Africa, the Sussexes made two major announcements in October 2019: Meghan had filed a lawsuit against the *Mail on Sunday* for printing extracts of a private letter she sent to her father in August 2018. And, Meghan and Harry said they were taking six weeks off their royal duties to spend some private time together as a family with their then-five-month-old son Archie.

The Sussexes opted to spend the holidays of 2020 on Vancouver Island, Canada, instead of the typical royal Christmas at Sandringham, then returned to the UK on January 6, 2020. Then, on January 8, one day after a visit to Canada House in London, the Sussexes dropped a surprise announcement: They launched their website, SussexRoyal.com, through which they revealed they'd be stepping back as senior members of the royal family, cutting themselves off from the Sovereign Grant in an aim to be financially independent, and splitting their time between North America and the UK.

"After many months of reflection and internal discussions, we have chosen to make a transition this year in starting to carve out a progressive new role within this institution," a statement released by the couple read. "We intend to step back as 'senior' members of the Royal Family and work to become financially independent, while continuing to fully support Her Majesty The Queen."

But the announcement was forcibly rushed out due to leaks within the palace: The day before, on January 7, the *Sun* posted a story about how the couple planned to spend more time in Canada. And while Harry had reportedly already emailed his father and grandmother about his and Meghan's decision to step down, he hadn't been able to meet with them in person about it, since a secretary told the couple the Queen's schedule wouldn't allow it until January 29, according to *Finding Freedom* by Omid Scobie and Carolyn Durand.

On January 13, Prince Harry got his chance: He met with the Queen, Prince Charles, and Prince William at what is now referred to as the Sandringham Summit. The group discussed the couple's plans and how to feasibly (and legally) make a split role work. After the meeting, the Queen released a statement.

"Today my family had very constructive discussions on the future of my grandson and his family," the Queen's message read. "My family and I are entirely supportive of Harry and Meghan's desire to create a new life as a young family. Although we would have preferred them to remain full-time working Members of the Royal Family, we respect and understand their wish to live a more independent life as a family while remaining a valued part of my family."

It was decided there would be a one-year transition period for the Sussexes starting on March 31, 2020, during which they would no longer be working members of the royal family. They'd also lose their ability to use their HRH titles or the word "royal"—so goodbye shiny new SussexRoyal.com website.

Also, Harry's honorary military appointments would be removed. The emotional blow of this decision was evident during one of their last events as senior working royals, when they received a standing ovation at the Mountbatten Festival of Music at the Royal Albert Hall on March 7. Harry, in his red military dress uniform during his last appearance as Captain General of the Royal Marines, held Meghan's hand tight and looked to fight back tears as the couple were applauded by the crowd.

The Sussexes are full steam ahead with Archewell, their post-royal rebrand. But what does that encapsulate— and what was their original intention when they quit the royal clan?

Sussex Royal, no more. What began on April 2, 2019, with the launch of the @SussexRoyal Instagram account, ended with a new beginning. Almost exactly one year later, Archewell was announced as Harry and Meghan's new charitable and creative venture.

On January 2, 2021, the Archewell website was born, and showcased Harry and Meghan's plans for their organization. Archewell currently consists of three parts: the Archewell Foundation (the Sussexes' philanthropic endeavors, including projects and partnerships with World Central Kitchen, the Loveland Foundation, and UCLA's Center for Critical Internet Inquiry), Archewell Audio (their multiyear Spotify partnership), and Archewell Productions (their Netflix deal that includes both scripted and unscripted content for the streaming platform, estimated to be worth over $100 million).

"At Archewell, we unleash the power of compassion to drive systemic cultural change. We do this through our nonprofit work within Archewell Foundation 501(c)(3), in addition to creative activations through the business verticals of audio and production," the site reads.

But that wasn't always the plan. Despite their announcement in January 2020 that their aim was to become "financially independent, while continuing to fully support Her Majesty The Queen" after stepping down from their roles as senior royals, Meghan and Harry said they didn't originally intend to produce content. The Spotify and Netflix deals were "never a part of the plan," Harry told Oprah during their interview. "We didn't have a plan. That was suggested by somebody else, by the point where my family literally cut me off financially, and I had to afford security for us."

Since then, the pair has announced two Netflix shows (*Heart of Invictus* and animated kids' show *Pearl*) and released their first Archewell Audio podcast episode on Spotify.

Meghan Markle and Prince Harry chose to announce they were pregnant with their second child on Valentine's Day 2021, a date that holds special significance for Prince Harry. Why?

On February 14, 2021, the Duke and Duchess of Sussex revealed they were expecting their second child. The date is special for Prince Harry: It's the same day that, thirty-seven years before, the press revealed Princess Diana, who was twenty-two at the time, was pregnant with him.

Flashback to 1984: Princess Diana's pregnancy with her second child was announced by Buckingham Palace on February 13 and was front page news on Valentine's Day. The betting odds heavily favored a girl, with the queen being quoted as "delighted" and Charles having "no preference whether it's a boy or girl" according to an archived edition of the *Daily Express*. Harry was born almost exactly seven months later, on September 15, 1984.

The Sussexes' second pregnancy news came after a monumental heartbreak for the couple: Meghan revealed she had miscarried the previous July in an op-ed titled "The Losses We Share," published in the *New York Times* on November 30, 2020.

"It was a July morning that began as ordinarily as any other day: Make breakfast. Feed the dogs. Take vitamins. Find that missing sock. Pick up the rogue crayon that rolled under the table. Throw my hair in a ponytail before getting my son from his crib," Meghan wrote. "After changing his diaper, I felt a sharp cramp. I dropped to the floor with him in my arms, humming a lullaby to keep us both calm, the cheerful tune a stark contrast to my sense that something was not right. I knew, as I clutched my firstborn child, that I was losing my second. Hours later, I lay in a hospital bed, holding my husband's hand. I felt the clamminess of his palm and kissed his knuckles, wet from both our tears. Staring at the cold white walls, my eyes glazed over. I tried to imagine how we'd heal."

Meghan Markle and Prince Harry now live in California, where they're raising their son and daughter, two dogs, and what other animal?

*A*n estate in Montecito, California, is the home of British royalty...and chickens. Specifically, rescue chickens from a factory farm, which made their world debut during the Sussexes' Oprah interview. "She's always wanted chickens," Harry told Oprah. "I just love rescuing," Meghan added. The best part: The chickens live in a red coop that's painted with the name "Archie's Chick Inn" on the grounds of Meghan and Harry's estate.

After a temporary stay in the swanky Beverly Hills digs loaned to them by movie producer Tyler Perry, Harry and Meghan purchased their home, an 18,671-square-foot Mediterranean-style residence that was listed at $14.65 million in the summer of 2020. The property is located on a gated street in the celeb-studded enclave of Montecito, which is 90 miles from LA and about a stone's throw from Santa Barbara. The home has nine bedrooms and sixteen bathrooms, plus a guesthouse, playset for the children, teahouse, swimming pool, gym, sauna, tennis court—and now chicken coop—on the 7.5-acre grounds.

Raising chickens is just the start. It's clear the family of four are enjoying their newfound freedom via video clips shared during their interview with Oprah of Harry and Meghan on the beach playing fetch with their two dogs, Pula and Guy; Harry swinging in the backyard with Archie; their Christmas card featuring Archie's wooden playhouse; Harry going bike riding with his son. "One word to describe their new life in California?" Oprah asked. "Peace," Meghan answered, saying the best part was "being able to live authentically. It's so basic, but it's really ful-filling. Just getting back down to basics."

Even before their fairy tale wedding, Meghan Markle was plagued by racist media coverage, including headlines like "Straight Outta Compton" and being described in an article as having "exotic" DNA. But the couple claims to have also faced racism within the Firm surrounding one major milestone. What was it?

During the couple's ITV interview while on tour of southern Africa, Meghan said she never expected royal life to be easy, "but I expected it to be fair." She said she'd been warned about the relentless media scrutiny by her inner circle. When she met Harry, she told interviewer Tom Bradby, "My friends were really happy because I was so happy, but my British friends said to me, 'I'm sure he's great but you shouldn't do it because the British tabloids will destroy your life.' And I, very naively—I'm American," continued Markle. "We don't have that there—[I said], 'What are you talking about? That doesn't make any sense. I'm not in any tabloids.' I didn't get it. So it's been, yeah, it's been complicated."

She touched on the topic again in her and Harry's Oprah interview, comparing criticism of the Duchess of Cambridge to the critiques printed about herself. "Kate was called 'Waity Katie,' waiting to marry William," she said. "While I imagine that was really hard—and I do, I can't picture what that felt like—this is not the same. And if a member of his family will comfortably say, 'We've all had to deal with things that are rude…' Rude and racist are not the same. And equally, you've also had a press team that goes on the record to defend you, especially when they know something's not true. And that didn't happen for us."

Harry reiterated that the couple hadn't received help from within the palace during *The Me You Can't See* docuseries. "Every single ask, request, warning, whatever it is, to stop just got met with total silence or total neglect," he told cohost Oprah, referring to asking his family and their team for help against the attacks the couple were facing online. "We spent four years trying to make it work. We did everything that we possibly could to stay there and carry on doing the role and doing the job."

But it wasn't just the press that scrutinized the couple. Perhaps the biggest bombshell to come out of the Oprah interview was that a member of the royal family raised "concerns and conversations about how dark [Archie's] skin might be."

Harry had been in "several conversations" with "family" on the topic, said Meghan. "About how dark your baby is going to be?" asked a shocked-face Oprah. "Potentially," Meghan answered, "and what that would mean or look like." Meghan declined to name the person who raised the concerns: "I think that would be very damaging to them." But Oprah followed up the day after the interview aired, during *CBS This Morning*, to clarify that the couple told her that the conversation about Archie's skin was not raised by Queen Elizabeth or Prince Philip.

Both Meghan Markle and Prince Harry won major lawsuits against the press in 2020, one of which was predicated on a letter Meghan wrote to whom?

A letter Meghan wrote to her father, Thomas Markle, before her wedding to Prince Harry became the subject of a massive lawsuit against publisher Associated Newspapers that lasted nearly two years. She sued the publisher of the *Mail on Sunday* for invasion of privacy and copyright infringement after the paper printed excerpts of Meghan's letter in five articles starting in February 2019.

The High Court judge presiding over her case, Justice Mark Warby, ruled in the duchess's favor in February 2021. He said that the publisher had misused Meghan's private information and infringed her copyright and that she "had a reasonable expectation that the contents of the letter would remain private" and concluded the paper's publication of large chunks of it was "manifestly excessive and hence unlawful."

Prince Harry also won a lawsuit against the *Mail on Sunday* in 2021, this time over an article published in October 2020 that claimed the former Captain General of the Royal Marines had "turned his back" on his treasured military associations and ignored a letter from Lord Dannatt, a former Chief of the General Staff, that requested more support for the British military community. The paper printed an apology, issued a correction, and paid the duke "significant damages," which he then donated to the Invictus Games.

Before Archie was born, it was said that his parents did not want to give their son a title. Instead, he will be known as what?

*M*aster Archie, coming through. At just two years old, Master Archie has already accomplished more than we have in our lifetime (kidding, kind of...). In 2019, on his first overseas royal tour, he met Archbishop Desmond Tutu. He and Meghan also (virtually) joined Jennifer Garner, Reese Witherspoon, and other megacelebs to read a book for charity, had a cameo in his parents' first podcast episode ("Happy...new...year!"), and appeared on CBS in a family beach video aired during the Sussexes' Oprah interview.

But even before he was born, there was already controversy. While it was widely reported Meghan and Harry did not want to give Archie a title in order to protect him from a life in the spotlight, the Sussexes revealed during the Oprah interview that, actually, they weren't offered the option.

"How did they explain to you that your son, the great-grandson of the Queen, wasn't going to be a prince?" Oprah asked Meghan. "You certainly must have had some conversations with Harry about it and had your own suspicions as to why they didn't want to make Archie a prince. Why do you think that is?"

"They didn't want him to be a prince...which would be different from protocol, and that he wasn't going to receive security..." Meghan responded. "We have in tandem the conversation of, 'He won't be given security. He's not going to be given a title.' And also concerns and conversations about how dark his skin might be when he's born," she continued.

The fallout from the interview sent shock waves through the UK, and the queen released an unprecedented statement saying that the whole family was "saddened" to learn how challenging Harry and Meghan's last few years had been. It also said that "while some recollections may vary, they are taken very seriously and will be addressed by the family privately. Harry, Meghan, and Archie will always be much-loved family members."

Prince Harry has continued to focus on mental health activism since stepping down from his senior royal role. He candidly discussed his own mental health struggles on what popular celebrity podcast?

*W*elcome back to *Armchair Expert* with actor/comedian/director Dax Shepard and Emmy-nominated producer Monica Padman. Fans of the long-form conversational podcast were in for a royal treat as Prince Harry joined for an episode in May 2021. During the 90-minute episode, Harry opened up about everything, from tech algorithms and the tabloids to his time in the military and watching his mum get chased by the paparazzi.

As far as royal life, Harry described it like a "mixture between *The Truman Show* and being in a zoo." He continued: "It's the job right? Grin and bear it. Get on with it. I was in my early twenties, and I was thinking I don't want this job, I don't want to be here. I don't want to be doing this. Look what it did to my mum. How am I ever going to settle down and have a wife and family, when I know it's going to happen again? I've seen behind the curtain, I've seen the business model and seen how this whole thing works, and I don't want to be part of this," he added.

When asked about fatherhood, Harry replied, "Certainly, when it comes to parenting, if I've experienced some form of pain or suffering because of the pain or suffering that perhaps my father or my parents had suffered, I'm going to make sure that I break that cycle, so that I don't pass it on, basically. There's a lot of genetic pain and suffering that gets passed on anyway. As parents we should be doing the most we can to try and say, 'You know what, that happened to me, I'm going to make sure that doesn't happen to you.'"

Harry, speaking about his dad, added: "I also know that's connected to his parents. So that means that he's treating me the way that he was treated, which means how can I change that for my own kids? And well, here I am. I've now moved my whole family to the US. That wasn't the plan. Sometimes you've got to make decisions, and put your family first and your mental health first."

He also touched on his rom-com moment with Meghan at a supermarket, unlearning unconscious bias, what drove him to seek therapy ("It was a conversation that I had with my now-wife," he said. "She saw it. She saw it straight away. She could tell that I was hurting and that some of the stuff that was out of my control was making me really angry. It would make my blood boil."), what it was like growing up royal, and his position of privilege.

Remember: Harry also founded Heads Together—the mental health initiative of the Royal Foundation—with William and Kate back in 2016. And Harry's appearance on the *Armchair Expert* podcast wasn't the only continuation of his aim to break down the stigma surrounding mental health and wellness. He also partnered with Oprah to produce and star in the Apple TV+ docuseries *The Me You Can't See*, which debuted on the streaming platform in May 2021. And he added a new title to his post-royal résumé in March 2021: Chief Impact Officer of BetterUp, a Silicon Valley startup for app-based mental fitness, professional development, coaching, and counseling.

On June 4, 2021, Meghan Markle and Prince Harry welcomed their second child, a baby girl. They named their daughter after the Queen, but her name's not Elizabeth. What is it?

Welcome, Lilibet Diana Mountbatten-Windsor! Harry and Meghan's daughter was born at 11:40 a.m. on June 4 at Santa Barbara Cottage Hospital in Santa Barbara, California. She is eighth in the line of succession. The official statement from the royal couple was made on June 6, meaning the parents had a few days of blissful quiet before the media were alerted to baby Lilibet's arrival. "Both mother and child are healthy and well, and settling in at home," the announcement read.

The statement also revealed the baby would go by "Lili." So how did the new parents choose their daughter's name? We know that Lilibet was Queen Elizabeth's childhood nickname, mainly because Elizabeth is a pretty tricky name for a two-year-old to pronounce. When guests visited, the way then-Princess Elizabeth introduced herself sounded a lot like "Lilibet." The nickname stuck—she would soon sign her private correspondence "Love from Lilibet." Prince Philip even adopted the moniker for her and in a note to the Queen Mother in 1947, wrote, "Lilibet is the only 'thing' in the world that is absolutely real to me."

The baby's second name is an obvious homage to Harry's mother, who was actually named after Diana Russell, Duchess of Bedford, of the 18th century, who *also* went by Lady Diana Spencer. The story goes that Diana's parents were eagerly awaiting a boy, then struggled to find a girl name when Diana arrived. The irony: The eighteenth century Diana was also set up with the then-Prince of Wales (but it didn't work out, and Diana went on to marry the Duke of Bedford).

An update posted to their Archewell website revealed the Sussexes' unbridled joy: "On June 4th, we were blessed with the arrival of our daughter, Lili. She is more than we could have ever imagined, and we remain grateful for the love and prayers we've felt from across the globe. Thank you for your continued kindness and support during this very special time for our family." The couple finished by asking that in lieu of gifts, well-wishers could support or learn more about four organizations focused on working with women and girls: Girls Inc., Harvest Home, CAMFED, or Myna Mahila Foundation.

But the British media had a field day. How could Harry and Meghan pay homage to the queen with her beloved family nickname while publicly calling out the Firm? One particular article, citing a palace source, alleged the queen had no prior knowledge before the baby's name was announced to the public. The Sussexes hit back, releasing a statement (along with legal warnings) in response to the rumors: "The Duke spoke with his family in advance of the announcement, in fact his grandmother was the first family member he called. During that conversation, he shared their hope of naming their daughter Lilibet in her honor." The spokesperson added, "Had she not been supportive, they would not have used the name."

Prince Harry will join other royals like the Duke of Windsor and the Duchess of York by writing what?

*M*eghan joined the royal ranks of Prince Charles and Sarah Ferguson in penning a children's book. Titled *The Bench*, it contains a poem she wrote for Harry on his first Father's Day, about the special bond between fathers and sons, and was released in June 2021. Now Harry is on his own path to authorship.

Prince Harry will release a biography in the fall of 2022, according to a press release from the publisher, Penguin Random House. The memoir is being ghostwritten by Pulitzer Prize–winning journalist and novelist J. R. Moehringer, and the proceeds from the book will go to charity.

"In an intimate and heartfelt memoir from one of the most fascinating and influential global figures of our time, Prince Harry will share, for the very first time, the definitive account of the experiences, adventures, losses, and life lessons that have helped shape him," the statement read. The book will cover "his lifetime in the public eye from childhood to the present day, including his dedication to service, the military duty that twice took him to the frontlines of Afghanistan, and the joy he has found in being a husband and father."

Harry added, "I'm writing this not as the prince I was born but as the man I have become. I've worn many hats over the years, both literally and figuratively, and my hope is that in telling my story—the highs and lows, the mistakes, the lessons learned—I can help show that no matter where we come from, we have more in common than we think. I'm deeply grateful for the opportunity to share what I've learned over the course of my life so far and excited for people to read a firsthand account of my life that's accurate and wholly truthful."

But he's not the first royal family member to write a biography. While both Princess Diana's story—written by Andrew Morton and based on audio interviews with the princess—and Prince Charles's authorized biography by Jonathan Dimbleby were written by other people, plenty of other royals have penned their own. Sarah Ferguson published two autobiographies, *My Story* and *Finding Sarah*, while the Duke of Windsor published *A King's Story* in 1951, fifteen years after his abdication.

PART III

PRINCESS DIANA

Diana was the fourth of five children born to John, 8th Earl Spencer, and Frances Shand Kydd (formerly Frances Ruth Roche). Who was the most famous guest that attended their wedding?

*F*irst came Sarah (born in 1955), then came Jane (born in 1957), followed by John (Diana's older brother, he was born in 1960, but he died just ten hours after childbirth). Then, there was Diana Frances Spencer, who entered the world on July 1, 1961, at Park House near Sandringham Estate in Norfolk, a nine-bedroom home her family leased from Queen Elizabeth II and the place she lived until her grandfather passed away and her father inherited his earldom in 1975.

Diana's dad—then the Viscount Althorp—actually served as equerry to King George VI from 1950 to 1952 and to Queen Elizabeth II from 1952 to 1954 after her father passed away. In fact, when John Spencer married Diana's mother (the daughter of Maurice Roche, 4th Baron Fermoy, and with more wealth than the Spencers) in 1954, Queen Elizabeth II herself attended as the "chief guest" for the ceremony at Westminster Abbey.

Still, Diana's parents' marriage didn't stay happy for long. At the time of Diana's arrival, her mother was still devastated at the loss of John, and the pressure to produce a male heir was real. When Diana (their fourth born...and another girl) arrived, it took her parents seven days to choose a name. (She was eventually named after Diana Russell, the Duchess of Bedford, a distant relative.)

Of course, Diana's brother Charles—now the 9th Earl Spencer—arrived in 1964 (Queen Elizabeth II was named as his godmother), but by then Diana's parents' marriage was already on the rocks. They separated in 1967 and divorced in 1969 when Diana was just seven years old and after Diana's mother fell in love with a wallpaper tycoon by the name of Peter Shand Kydd. A custody battle and bitter split ensued. Diana's brother Charles described the repercussions of this to the *Sunday Times* in 2020: "Our father was a quiet and constant source of love, but our mother wasn't cut out for maternity. Not her fault, she couldn't do it. She was in love with someone else—infatuated, really. While she was packing her stuff to leave, she promised Diana [then aged five] she'd come back to see her. Diana used to wait on the doorstep for her, but she never came." (Diana's dad eventually won full custody of the kids.)

Diana was born at Sandringham, a stone's throw from the residences of her future royal in-laws. Where did she move to next?

*W*hen Diana's dad, John, 8th Earl Spencer, inherited his earldom in 1975, he relocated his family from Park

House to Althorp House, a ninety-room estate located in the English countryside in Northamptonshire. Diana's distant ancestor, Sir John Spencer, had bought the estate in 1508, and the footprint of the mansion was later expanded in 1790. (The main house is currently estimated at 100,000 square feet.) The Althorp Estate in its entirety spans 13,000 acres of land.

When Diana was growing up, she was known to treasure her time on the estate. In sync with their new titles and residence, Diana's father simultaneously remarried in 1976. The woman was socialite Raine McCorquodale and, although her relationship with Diana was said to have improved by the end, Diana—a teenager at the time—was known to be less than happy with her father's choice. Diana and her siblings were said to have referred to her as "Acid Raine," but ahead of Raine's passing in 2016, she told *Gentlewoman* magazine: "[Diana] had incredibly heavy pressures put upon her, but we ended up huge friends. She used to come and sit on my sofa and tell me her troubles. I'm very happy about that." (Diana's mother also remarried in 1969 to the man she met during the latter part of her marriage to John, Peter Shand Kydd.)

Currently, Diana's brother Charles Spencer owns the estate after inheriting it in 1992 and often shares photos of it on his public Instagram account. It's also the site of Diana's final resting place.

Before Diana became the Princess of Wales, she had another title and a foretelling nickname assigned to her by her family—what were they and how did she earn them?

Although Diana entered the world as the Honorable Diana Frances Spencer, when her grandfather passed away and her father was named the 8th Earl Spencer, Diana inherited a new title: Lady Diana. Yes, she was technically a commoner when she wed Prince Charles in 1981, but Diana was no stranger to the finer ways of life. She came from nobility and an aristocratic family five hundred years in the making.

A bit of background about the Spencer family. They originally earned their fortune from sheep farming and wool trading. Still, it wasn't until one of Diana's ancestors acquired a title in the early 1600s that a Spencer was granted an earldom—and this led to real influence down the line. It also meant that Diana was raised with many of life's finer things including a governess, cook, and butler, all of whom had their own cottages in which to live.

Diana's ancestry also includes some pretty famous women. Namely, there's Sarah Churchill, Duchess of Marlborough—Queen Anne's confidante, played by Rachel Weisz in the film *The Favourite*—and Georgiana, Duchess of Devonshire, who was portrayed by Keira Knightley in *The Duchess*.

As for her nickname growing up, Diana was often called "Duch," due to her propensity to act like, well, a duchess. The nickname supposedly stuck around into adulthood, particularly with members of the Spencer clan. But Diana was assigned another nickname by the press when she started dating Prince Charles at the age of nineteen: "Shy Di." According to her brother Charles, Diana was a lot of things, but shy wasn't one of them. "She was never shy, but she was canny about people, and she was reserved to start with," he explained in an interview with *People* magazine.

Diana wasn't the best student and dropped out of school at age sixteen to pursue another passion. What was it?

*A*t the age of nine, Diana was sent to an all-girls boarding school called Riddlesworth in Norfolk, England, before enrolling at West Heath Girls' School near Kent at the age of twelve. But school wasn't for her. She failed her O-level exams (an assessment that was used as a pre-qualifier for A-levels—a route into higher education) twice, then dropped out of school entirely when she turned sixteen.

It was then that Diana enrolled in Institut Alpin Videmanette, a fancy all-girls Swiss finishing school whose famous alums include not only Diana's sister Sarah, but Prince William and Prince Harry's eventual nanny, Tiggy Legge-Bourke. Diana spent her days pursuing her many passions: swimming, skiing, tennis, and piano. But more than anything, Diana had her sights set on becoming a ballerina. Her height (5'10") was said to have worked against her. Still, in the late 1970s—when Diana was seventeen and back in the UK—she reached out to the Vacani School of Dance (a school that, at one point, gave private lessons to Princesses Elizabeth and Margaret) and briefly studied and taught ballet.

Despite the fact that she wasn't destined to be a ballerina, dance—of all kinds—was always a big part of Diana's life and long considered a stress buster for the princess when times were tough. Some of her more famous (albeit impromptu) performances include the time she twirled around a ballroom to the sounds of *Saturday Night Fever*. Also, the moment she surprised Charles for his thirty-seventh birthday, also in 1985, with a performance of Billy Joel's "Uptown Girl" at the Royal Opera House.

Princess Diana also met Prince Charles at the age of sixteen—but she spent quite a bit of time around his family before that. Why?

As a result of her upbringing at Park House at Sandringham—and the fact that Diana's father was Queen

Mary's godson and her maternal grandmother was lady-in-waiting to Queen Elizabeth the Queen Mother, among numerous other royal ties—Diana had a number of reasons to socialize with Queen Elizabeth II and her family whenever they were "in town." This led to plenty of time spent with Prince Andrew and Prince Edward (Charles's younger brothers, who were born in 1960 and 1964, respectively, and similar in age to Diana) as an adolescent. Tina Brown did reveal that Diana likely met Charles earlier than age sixteen, explaining in her book *The Diana Chronicles* that when Charles was just seventeen (and Diana only five years old), he walked in on a tea party she was having with Andrew.

Before Diana met Prince Charles, what did she do for work?

*A*gain, Diana was a member of a well-to-do family—she didn't need to work. But the princess-to-be spent her time taking on odd jobs like cleaning houses, working as a server at cocktail parties, and being a nanny. (One of her more well-known gigs was babysitting for the son of an American businesswoman named Mary Robertson, who went on to pen the book *The Diana I Knew: Loving Memories of the Friendship Between an American Mother and Her Son's Nanny Who Became the Princess of Wales*.)

Just ahead of dating Prince Charles, Diana was living in a London flat (an eighteenth birthday gift from her parents) with three roommates and working part-time as a kindergarten teacher at Young England Kindergarten in London's Pimlico district, a position she held for a couple of years. It was, in fact, Diana's last "normal" job. In an interview with the *Chicago Tribune* in 1997, the school's headmistress at the time, Kay King, revealed that Diana worked three afternoons a week, teaching painting, drawing, and dancing to approximately fifty children at the school. (Approached by the press in 1980, Diana explained the reason she performed the job: "I adore children—that's really why.") The school was also the scene of one of Diana's most famous photographs, a toddler on each hip with the bright sunlight shining through her white skirt—her introduction to the world ahead of her engagement to Charles.

And about her London flat… It was located at Coleherne Court, a block of apartments near Kensington where Diana lived with friends between 1979 and 1981. Her brother Charles described the address as "such a very happy place for Diana." In fact, as of 2021, a commemorative blue plaque commissioned by English Heritage, which manages more than four hundred sites and historic monuments in the UK, has been installed to honor Diana's former home.

Diana and Prince Charles had quite the whirlwind courtship, only meeting thirteen times before getting engaged. On what occasion did they first connect romantically?

*B*efore Diana, Charles was actually thought to be a great match with Diana's older sister Sarah. But his romantic involvement with Sarah didn't last long—the pair dated only briefly in 1977. (Apparently, Charles had quite a few girl-friends—some count as many as twenty—over the years as he attempted to move on from his on-again, off-again romance with Camilla Shand, who married Andrew Parker Bowles in 1973.) Still, it was during his courtship with Sarah—and a grouse hunt that he attended at the Althorp Estate—that Diana and Charles officially reconnected. (Charles spoke of the occasion in their engagement interview in 1981: "I remember thinking what a very jolly and amusing and attractive sixteen-year-old she was. I mean, great fun, and bouncy and full of life and everything.") After his relationship with Sarah ended, a few years went by before he reconnected with Diana in 1980 at a friend's home in Sussex.

At the time, Charles was in a particularly vulnerable state fol-lowing the death of Lord Mountbatten, the maternal uncle of Prince Philip and a person long-considered a friend and mentor to Charles. (Mountbatten was killed in a terrorist attack carried out by the Irish Republican Army in August of 1979.) Diana herself spoke of the timing of her reunion with Charles in an interview recorded in secret by her friend Dr. James Colthurst and later used in the Andrew Morton biography, *Diana: Her True Story*: "I said [to Charles]: 'You looked so sad when you walked up the aisle at Lord Mountbatten's funeral.' I said: 'It was the most tragic thing I've ever seen. My heart bled for you when I watched.' I thought: 'It's wrong, you're lonely—you should be with somebody to look after you.' The next minute he leapt on me practically and I thought this was all very strange…" Per Diana, that's when Charles's romantic interest in her bloomed—he was quite smitten, despite their twelve-year age difference. (Diana was nineteen; Charles was thirty-two.)

They spent their courtship talking mostly over the phone and met just thirteen times (over the course of six months) before getting engaged, Diana later revealed. All throughout, the press intrusion into her life was constant. The *New York Times* remarked upon the news of her engagement: "[Diana] blushes engagingly whenever she is sighted by the posse of press photographers who have been pursuing her for months." Then, "During the ordeal of pursuit to which Fleet Street reporters have subjected her in recent months, she has shown good humor and patience, although once, surprised by photographers at the wheel of her red Mini Metro, she burst into tears."

Still, their engagement was made official in February 1981, not long after Diana had been invited to join Charles for what was considered a fateful weekend with the royal family at Balmoral in November 1980.

Prince Charles proposed right before Diana embarked on a trip to Australia. She also picked out her own engagement ring. How come?

*T*iming is everything, as they say. With Diana set to leave for Australia with her mother in early February 1981, Charles decided to seize the moment and pop the question while the pair were in the nursery at Windsor Castle on February 3. He explained his reasoning in an interview with BBC Radio: "She had planned to go to Australia quite a long time before anyway with her mother, and I thought, 'Well, I'll ask her then so that she'll have a chance of thinking it over when she's away and saying I can't bear the whole idea or not,' as the case may be." But apparently, Diana didn't need to wait: She said yes to Charles right away. In their engagement interview, Diana said, "Oh, I never had any doubts about it."

The conversation went like this, according to Diana via interviews for Andrew Morton's *Diana: Her True Story*: "He said, 'Will you marry me?' and I laughed. I remember thinking, this is a joke and I said, 'Yeah, okay,' and laughed. He was deadly serious."

Diana's sister Sarah was thrilled to take some of the credit, at the time describing herself as "cupid" and reportedly saying, "He met Miss Right, and she met Mr. Right. They just clicked. They have the same giggly sense of humor and they both love ballet and opera and sport in all forms. It's perfect, and they are both over the moon about it."

The engagement ring—a twelve-carat Ceylon sapphire surrounded by fourteen solitaire diamonds, now worn by her daughter-in-law Kate Middleton—was something Diana herself chose out of a selection of options presented to her by Garrard, the Crown Jeweller from 1843 to 2007. Supposedly, the ring's design was inspired by a Garrard sapphire-and-diamond brooch given to Queen Victoria by her husband Albert just ahead of their wedding. In fact, Victoria even wore it as her "something blue" on her wedding day. Still, Diana is rumored to have loved the Marguerite ring because it reminded her of her mother's engagement ring.

The option to select the ring herself was thought to be the marker of a modern royal bride, but the move was later met with controversy once it was discovered that the ring Diana chose—which cost approximately $60,000 at the time—was actually a catalog option, meaning anyone with that amount of cash could walk into Garrard and buy themselves the same thing.

During their engagement interview, what line did Prince Charles famously utter that gave Diana pause?

*I*t was the one-liner heard 'round the world. During Diana and Charles's engagement interview following news of his proposal and her acceptance, a journalist asked the couple if they could find the words to sum up how they were feeling. He then asked: "And I suppose [you're] in love?" Diana replied immediately: "Of course." But Charles awkwardly added: "Whatever 'in love' means."

Although some have said this was the marker of Charles's philosophical mindset and exploration of the concept of marriage, it famously stirred doubt in Diana's mind at the time. Years later, she described this moment to Andrew Morton, author of *Diana: Her True Story*, saying, "This ridiculous [news] man said, 'Are you in love?' I thought, 'What a thick question.' So I said, 'Yes, of course, we are,' and Charles turned 'round and said, 'Whatever love means.' And that threw me completely. I thought, 'What a strange answer.' It traumatized me."

Of course, it also didn't help that Charles's affection for Camilla Parker Bowles was lurking in the background of Diana's entire courtship with the prince. The pair had been romantically linked in 1970 following a polo match at Windsor Great Park, but split after she married Andrew Parker Bowles in 1973. Still, their relationship continued.

While Charles's biographer says their affair began in 1986, Diana was tipped off to their relationship long before that, when she discovered a bracelet in Charles's possession days before their wedding, not for her, but for Camilla. The initials *G* and *F* were engraved. (Some say they stood for "Gladys" and "Fred," based on characters from *The Goon Show*, which Charles and Camilla were said to enjoy together; Charles's biographer—a well-known British journalist—Jonathan Dimbleby said they stood for "Girl Friday.")

Diana spoke of the incident in the tapes recorded for Andrew Morton's biography *Diana: Her True Story*: "The most awful thing had happened before [Charles] went," she said of Charles's tour of Australia and New Zealand in the weeks leading up to their wedding. "I was in his study talking to him about his trip. The telephone rang; it was Camilla...and then someone in his office told me that my husband had made a bracelet for her."

Later, Diana explained that she actually discovered the parcel containing the bracelet, but when she cried to her sisters about it, they told her she was in too deep. In Diana's words, they lovingly told her: "'Well, bad luck, Duch. Your face is on the tea towel. It's too late to back out now.'"

Princess Diana and Prince Charles bucked tradition and chose not to marry at Westminster Abbey. Where did they get married instead?

*F*ive months after announcing their engagement, Diana and Charles got married at St. Paul's Cathedral, a move that broke a centuries-old tradition of royal weddings being held at Westminster Abbey. (In fact, it had been 480 years since the last royal wedding at St. Paul's Cathedral, when Henry VII's son, Prince Arthur, married Catherine of Aragon on November 14, 1501.)

But Diana and Charles wanted their wedding to be different. In particular, Charles liked the fact that St. Paul's could hold a full orchestra and had a world-famous choir. They also needed a space that would accommodate the 3,500 guests in attendance. (Westminster Abbey only holds 2,200.)

Guests ranged from First Lady Nancy Reagan to Prime Minister Margaret Thatcher to Princess Grace of Monaco. Camilla and Andrew Parker Bowles were also present for Diana and Charles's big day and Diana invited the entire staff of the nursery school she worked for leading up to her engagement to Charles. Over 750 million people in seventy-four countries tuned in to watch Diana marry Charles on July 29, 1981, with

600,000 people lining the streets to wish them well. (A public holiday was declared.)

The large crowds meant the pressure was on for the princess. What line did Princess Diana famously flub in her vows?

Marrying a prince (and future king) in front of millions of people watching in person and at home around the world—no big deal, right? Diana, who was just twenty at the time, appeared poised and put together. The only sign that the future Princess of Wales was a touch nervous? She flip-flopped Charles's name while reciting her vows. Yep, Diana accidentally referred to Charles as Philip Charles Arthur George instead of Charles Philip Arthur George.

But she wasn't the only person to make a mistake: Charles also had a slipup, telling Diana he would offer her "thy goods" instead of "my worldly goods."

Those weren't the only royal wedding mishaps. According to Barbara Daly, Princess Diana's wedding-day makeup artist, Diana accidentally splashed perfume on her wedding gown, so much that it left a mark, while trying to dab on some of her favorite scent, Quelques Fleurs from Parisian perfume house

Houbigant. (Di covered it up by hiding the spot with her hand as she made her grand entrance at St. Paul's.)

In addition to that, one of Diana's bridesmaids, five-year-old Clementine Hambro (a former student of Diana's and great-granddaughter of Winston Churchill), tripped and fell and started crying after the ceremony. Diana apparently saved the day, scooping her up and asking: "Did you bump your bottom?"—a line that distracted Clementine from her tears.

Finally, it was the ultimate royal wedding "oops"—Diana and Charles forgot to seal their vows with a kiss. But they found a way to make up for it by kissing in public on the Buckingham Palace balcony as massive crowds cheered below. A new royal tradition was born.

Who designed Princess Diana's wedding dress—and recently revealed that, in case of royal emergency, there was a backup waiting in the wings?

*T*apped by Diana herself, David and Elizabeth Emanuel were the married (now divorced) dream team behind the fairy tale princess-worthy frock that she chose to wear down the aisle at St. Paul's Cathedral to marry Prince Charles on July 29, 1981. But the Princess of Wales didn't just call them out of the blue. She'd worked with the up-and-coming British designers on at least a few occasions prior to "I do" and felt a level of trust in their work, not to mention confidence that they were the right duo for her wedding and quest to prove herself a style icon. (Elizabeth recently told British *Vogue*, "Diana was still developing her sense of style at the time. She left it to us and our brand of new-romanticism.")

The finished look is Diana's ivory taffeta gown—one of the most iconic wedding dresses ever made—which featured ten thousand pearls and was intricately embroidered with sequins and frilled lace. The train, twenty-five feet in length, was the longest in royal history. (The dress was estimated to have been worth $115,000 at the time, although Elizabeth told British *Vogue* that they charged the royal family 1,000 guineas, a price her father came up with: "We would have given it to Diana for free, but that token amount seemed right, and my dad thought it would be romantic to use guineas.")

But almost as thrilling as being chosen to design the Princess of Wales's gown were the efforts that went into keeping it a secret ahead of the big day. The Emanuels have long described the massive media presence outside their design studio that began the second they signed on to work with Diana for the mega event. The pressure to keep everything hush-hush was so intense that they actually installed a safe as an extra precaution to hold sketches, fabric swatches, and details about the final silhouette. There's more: the Emanuels went so far as creating an alternate style (one with a much more pronounced V neckline and no lace along the skirt's hem) just in case the wedding dress design happened to be leaked.

Still, a royal mystery prevails: The second dress mysteriously vanished from the studio. Elizabeth recently told the *Daily Mail* she doesn't know what happened to it: "It was hanging up in the studio for a long time, and then it disappeared. I don't know if we sold it or put it into storage. It was such a busy time. I'm sure it will turn up in a bag one day!"

Princess Diana and Prince Charles's honeymoon took place on the Royal Yacht *Britannia*. But it wasn't a happy one. Why?

*R*eflecting back on her wedding in tapes recorded for Andrew Morton's biography *Diana: Her True Story*, Diana called her wedding day "the worst day of her life." (Charles later told friends, according to biographer Robert Jobson in *Charles At Seventy: Thoughts, Hopes and Dreams*: "I desperately wanted to get out of the wedding in 1981, when during the engagement I discovered just how awful the prospects were having had no chance whatsoever to get to know Diana beforehand.")

Add in Diana's bracelet discovery and Charles's daily phone calls to Camilla Parker Bowles (which continued on board), and it's clear why the occasion wasn't exactly blissful. By that early point, the pair felt worlds apart romantically, but also intellectually. According to sources, Charles—who was thirty-two—preferred to spend the honeymoon reading, painting, and sunning himself while Diana (just twenty years old) wanted to spend the days together talking. This led to many arguments aboard.

In addition to that, Diana also noticed Charles wearing a new pair of cuff links. She later told Andrew Morton for *Diana: Her True Story*: "On our honeymoon, cuff links arrive on his wrists. Two *C*s entwined like the Chanel *C*. Got it. One knew exactly. So I said, 'Camilla gave you those, didn't she?' He said, 'Yes, so what's wrong? They're a present from a friend.' And boy, did we have a row. Jealousy, total jealousy."

To make matters worse, Diana had been struggling with bulimia for quite some time. It actually started the week after she and Charles got engaged. "My husband put his hand on my waistline and said: 'Oh, a bit chubby here, aren't we?' and that triggered off something in me—and the Camilla thing." (According to Elizabeth Emanuel, who designed Diana's wedding gown, when Diana began dress fittings, her waist measured 26 to 27 inches, but was down to 23 inches by her wedding day.)

Still, the pair cruised around the Mediterranean for fourteen days visiting Gibraltar off the coast of Spain and the Greek Islands before ending at Balmoral Castle in Scotland.

When Princess Diana gave birth to her firstborn son, Prince William, it wasn't at Buckingham Palace. Where was it?

*J*ust three months after their wedding, Diana and Charles had news: She was pregnant with a baby, due to arrive in June. (The announcement came the day after an iconic image of the Princess of Wales asleep at the ball—er, a gala—dressed in a literal fairy-tale princess gown, an off-the-shoulder Bellville Sassoon design.)

Diana was a royal rule breaker in a lot of ways, but one of the more notable examples of that was the decision she and Charles made to deliver their firstborn son, Prince William, at St. Mary's Hospital in Paddington, London. The queen was said to have favored a delivery at Buckingham Palace—as was royal tradition for all of her children (except for Anne, who was born at Clarence House due to renovations at the palace)—but Diana and Charles preferred the now famous Lindo Wing. In choosing it, Diana became the first royal to give birth to a future monarch at a hospital versus at home. (Anne was the original rule breaker—she gave birth to her daughter, Zara Phillips, also at the Lindo Wing, on May 18, 1981.)

In doing so, Diana reset the royal precedent. (Flash forward thirty-one years, and Prince William and Kate Middleton followed in his mother's footsteps, delivering not only Prince George—an heir to the throne—at St. Mary's, but Princess Charlotte and Prince Louis, too.)

As for her pregnancy with Prince William, Diana revealed to Andrew Morton, author of *Diana: Her True Story*, that it was less than smooth. She struggled quite a bit with morning sickness, but also the challenges of her continued transition into royal life. When she was four months along, she told Morton, she was having such a hard time emotionally that she threw herself down a flight of stairs as a desperate cry for help. (Her stomach sustained a few bruises, but physically, she was fine.)

Diana went on to deliver Prince William Arthur Philip Louis ten days early on June 21, 1982. (Charles was present—the first heir apparent to witness his child's delivery since Queen Victoria's reign.) The media pressure around her delivery date got to be too much, and she was induced early. The *New York Times* explained it best upon her pregnancy announcement, saying that the hopes of a nation struggling with economic decline were all placed on Diana: "Today's news threatens to turn adulation into idolatry....a pregnant princess will be a vivid symbol of the continuity of the monarchy, with its links to the past and its promise of at least one element of stability in the future."

Princess Diana's first solo royal engagement overseas was a surprising one. What event did she attend?

*I*n September 1982, Diana represented the queen at the state funeral of Princess Grace of Monaco. (The former Grace Kelly died of a cerebral hemorrhage while driving along a winding road in the Cote d'Azur region of France, which led her to lose control of the vehicle and plunge down a forty-five-foot embankment.) Diana had always viewed Princess Grace as a bit of a kindred spirit. Upon learning the news of her untimely passing, she went straight to Prince Charles to let him know she'd like to attend.

The pair had apparently hit it off during Diana's first post-engagement public event, on the arm of Prince Charles. It was a music recital at Goldsmiths' Hall, and she chose a strapless black dress that left her feeling vulnerable and exposed. (Charles didn't help the situation either—he famously was taken aback that she'd chosen to wear black, a color traditionally reserved for periods of mourning.) But Grace took her aside and helped Diana feel more at ease.

Diana later explained the reason she wanted to attend the funeral in tapes recorded for Andrew Morton's *Diana: Her True Story*. "I said, 'Well, I think it's important because she was an outsider who married into a big family and I've done the same, so it would feel right.' So I went to the queen and I said: 'You know, I'd like to do this,' and she said: 'I don't see why not. If you want to do this, you can'... I went there, did my bit, came back and everyone was all over me like a bad rash: 'Oh, you did so well!' And I thought: 'Well, interesting.'"

Shortly after William's arrival, Princess Diana and Prince Charles embarked on their first overseas tour. Where did they go?

Australia and New Zealand. It was 1983 and the official kickoff to what would soon be known as Di Mania (which many described as akin to Beatlemania—the crowds, sometimes in the six figures, were that excited). But it was also known to be a tipping point in the Wales's marriage. The reason? It was crystal clear from the start that the royal star everyone came out to see was Diana, not Charles. There were even complaints overheard when crowds found themselves on Charles's side of the street instead of Diana's. Still, despite what is depicted in *The Crown*, their time down under was actually thought to be one of the more blissful periods during their marriage. Diana herself said of the six-week tour to Andrew Morton, author of *Diana: Her True Story*: "We were a family unit and everything was fine."

The choice to bring Prince William along did break royal tradition, but it wasn't met with as much internal pushback as reported. Per Diana, the prime minister of Australia was the one who suggested William join, and both Charles and Diana thought it was a nice idea. "We didn't see William very much but at least we were under the same sky, so to speak. That was a great fulfillment for me because everyone wanted to know about his progress," she told Morton. (It's true: William spent much of the time in Woomargama, an outback ranch in New South Wales, with his nanny Barbara Barnes. Diana and Charles could only join during breaks in their packed schedule.)

But William's inclusion turned out to also be a defining moment for the Princess of Wales since it solidified her image as doting "mum" and a royal figure who was more relatable and human than the rest. In fact, one of the pair's greatest joys during the tour, as Charles wrote to a friend in a letter uncovered by royal biographer Sally Bedell Smith in her book *Prince Charles: The Passions and Paradoxes of an Improbable Life*, was watching William crawl around "at high speed knocking everything off the tables and causing unbelievable destruction" as Diana and Charles watched and laughed with "sheer, hysterical pleasure."

Other major moments included Diana and Charles's hike up Ayers Rock—now called Uluru—and Diana's now controversial pause halfway up, thought to be due to weakness, but likely due to her realization that her button-up dress was ill suited for the trek and likely to blow open, according to news reports. Another iconic scene from the tour (and one that cemented Diana and Charles as oh-so-in-love in the eyes of the public) was their romantic whirl around the ballroom at a charity event in Sydney. Overall, the trip was deemed a major success.

When Princess Diana announced she was pregnant with her second child, what holiday did the announcement coincide with?

*I*ntentionally or not, Diana and Charles—via Buckingham Palace—shared the news that they were expecting (again) on the evening of February 13, 1984, which meant the news hit the papers on a holiday synonymous with romance: Valentine's Day. (In fact, Prince Harry and Meghan Markle paid subtle tribute to Diana with the announcement on Valentine's Day 2021 that they were expecting their second child...a cool thirty-seven years since Harry's mother did it.)

Diana credited the six weeks leading up to the arrival of Henry Charles Albert David (Harry) on September 15, 1984, as the closest she ever was to Charles. But she also came to reveal to Andrew Morton, author of *Diana: Her True Story,* that she hid the fact that the baby was a he—not a she—since Charles was said to have desperately wanted a girl. Similar to her pregnancy with William, Diana suffered from morning sickness, but continued her public engagements until just six weeks before giving birth.

Of the delivery, Charles revealed in the hours after that it went much faster than her delivery with William. He also told crowds that his new son had pale blue eyes and hair of "an intermittent color" before cracking a joke about the addition saying, "we've nearly got a full polo team now."

Princess Diana was hell-bent on giving her kids a nonroyal upbringing. How did she pull this off?

For Diana, some of the happiest moments of her life were those that came as part of the role she prioritized above all else: mum. In addition to bringing Prince William along to Australia, she went out of her way to expose her sons to the real world, even if their version always included a security detail. Among the choices she made on behalf of William and Harry? William became the first heir to the throne to attend public school. She took them both to the movies, amusement parks, and to McDonald's, too. She even did the school drop-off and pickup and participated in school events (including running barefoot in a race against other mothers at Wetherby School in 1991), something unheard of for royal mothers at the time.

ROYAL TRIVIA

She also exposed them to the hardships of life, bringing them along with her to engagements at hospitals and homeless shelters at a very young age.

Prince Harry reflected on the impact of his mother's approach to parenting in the documentary *Diana, Our Mother: Her Life and Legacy* saying she was the "best mum in the world" and someone who "would just engulf you and squeeze you as tight as possible. And being as short as I was then, there was no escape. You were there for as long as she wanted to hold you.

"Shy Di," "Dynasty Di," "Lady Di," and "Queen of Hearts" were all nicknames given to the Princess of Wales. Which moniker is Princess Diana most famously known as and why?

The British tabloids loved any chance for a good headline rhyme, pun, or wordplay (still do!), so much so that they even went for "Darling Di" and "Di-namite" in addition to those listed above. But the one nickname for Princess Diana that really stood the test of time? "The People's Princess."

However, the name didn't come from the media. It was first coined by then prime minister Tony Blair (who was just four months into his first term as PM) in the stirring speech he gave to a grieving nation mourning the tragic loss of Diana to a car crash.

On August 31, 1997, in front of St. Mary Magdalene Church before attending a service, Blair reflected on Diana's legacy. "She was a wonderful and warm human being. Though her own life was often sadly touched by tragedy, she touched the lives of so many others in Britain and throughout the world with joy and with comfort. How many times shall we remember her and in how many different ways with the sick, the dying, with children and the needy, when with just a look or a gesture...she would reveal to all of us the depth of her compassion and humanity."

"We know how difficult things were for her from time to time. I'm sure we can only guess at but the people everywhere... kept faith with Princess Diana. They like her, they loved her, they regarded her as one of the people. She was the people's princess and that's how she will stay, how she will remain in our hearts and in our memories forever."

The name stuck. It summed up Diana's humanitarian work in Africa, her compassion and care for AIDS patients and the homeless, her work with domestic-violence victims and those suffering from mental health problems—she was truly a princess of the people. But it also encapsulated the nation's love for the Princess of Wales: a princess the people loved and cherished, and were devastated to lose.

In the CNN docuseries *The Windsors*, royal correspondent Richard Kay said, "He coined this wonderful phrase about the people's princess and it struck a chord. It seemed to sum up the feelings of a country in a paralysis of grief and shock in a way that the queen did not do."

Princess Diana admitted to confronting Camilla Parker Bowles about her affair with Prince Charles in the secret tapes recorded for Andrew Morton's biography. What was Camilla's response, according to Diana?

A party, an affair, and a confrontation: the setting for a social disaster. But, according to Diana, it was a mature conversation—and one that she didn't regret. "One of the bravest moments of my entire ten years was when we went to a ghastly party, a fortieth birthday party for Camilla's sister, and nobody expected me to turn up," Diana revealed to Andrew Morton for *Diana: Her True Story*.

"But, again, a voice inside me said 'just go for the hell of it.' So I psyched myself up something awful. I decided I wasn't going to kiss Camilla hello anymore, I was going to shake hands with her. This was my big step."

After dinner, Diana noticed that Prince Charles and Camilla were both missing, so she went downstairs to find them (and another partygoer) chatting on the couch. "And I said, 'Camilla, I'd love to have a word with you if possible,' and she got really uncomfortable and put her head down and said, 'Oh yes, alright,' and I said to the two men, 'Okay boys, I'm just going to have a quick word with Camilla, and I'll be up in a minute,' and they shot upstairs like chickens with no heads, and I could feel upstairs all hell breaking loose, 'What is she going to do?'"

"I mean, I was terrified of her, and I said, 'Camilla, I would just like you to know that I know exactly what's going on.' She said, 'I don't know what you're talking about!' And I said, 'I know what's going on between you and Charles, and I just want you to know that.' And, very interesting, she said to me 'You've got everything you ever wanted. You've got all the men in the world falling in love with you, and you've got two beautiful children. What more could you want?' I didn't believe her, so I said, 'I want my husband.'"

"And she said, 'well,' and she looked down the whole time. And I said to Camilla, 'I'm sorry I'm in the way. I obviously am in the way and it must be hell for both of you. But I do know what's going on, don't treat me like an idiot.'"

"In the car on the way back, my husband was on me like a bad rash. I cried like I've never cried before. It was anger, seven years of pent-up anger coming out… I didn't sleep that night. But the next morning I woke up and I felt different—a shift. I'd done something, said what I felt. Still the old jealousy and anger swirling around, but it wasn't so deathly as it had been before."

ROYAL TRIVIA

Her childhood dream of becoming a ballerina might not have happened, but Princess Diana famously danced on stage for Prince Charles. What song did she dance to?

Although she was deemed too tall to be a professional ballerina (a childhood dream of hers), Diana loved to dance, and she did so in public a few times in her adult life (like at the White House—most famously with John Travolta—and during the couples' Australia tour). But who could forget about her "Uptown Girl" moment? The Princess of Wales twirled onstage at the Royal Opera House to the Billy Joel hit as a Christmas surprise for Prince Charles (although *The Crown* portrayed it as a birthday present).

In December 1985, four years into their marriage, Diana slipped out of the royal box midway through the charity performance and met up with Wayne Sleep, a Royal Ballet dancer. Sleep told *Vulture* that the two had choreographed their contemporary routine (including a lift, double pirouettes, and jazz hip rolls) in secret for weeks. Diana had picked out her outfit (a white satin drop-waist dress—"with a *whoosh* to it," Sleep recalls Diana telling him) and the song before they even started practicing.

The routine was a hit—something Sleep had worried about due to the difference in heights (the princess was 5'10"; he's

5'2"): "We brought the house down with humor because they didn't know what was coming next," Sleep said. "And at the end, we joined each other. It was almost like a chorus line and a kick line. Our legs got higher and higher." Diana even wanted to do an encore: "Everyone's mouths gaped open. There was an intake of breath like they couldn't believe it. The noise got bigger and bigger. We did eight curtain calls," Sleep recalled. "She wanted to do it again, and I said no. She loved it. I have the motto, *Leave them wanting more*." Also, Sleep recalled, he was worried that by the second time, cameras would be ready to film (there's no video of the original dance because no one knew it was coming).

But, was it a hit with everyone? According to some, Prince Charles was less than pleased. (Biographer Tina Brown wrote in *The Diana Chronicles*, "It was embarrassingly clear that he had not been ravished by the spectacle of his wife *en pointe*. His disappointing response, when it leaked, was interpreted as frigid disapproval of Diana's lapse in royal etiquette.") But Sleep recalls that, "Everything seemed fine. I think Diana thought, *'Just in case, I've got Wayne on my side.'* I'm going to keep my mouth closed on what it was like to be there. [Charles] had a raised eyebrow, you might say. It didn't go any further than that at the party."

What animal was featured on an item of clothing Princess Diana first wore to a polo match in 1980 that led to the item's massive surge in sales, became a symbol of Diana's unique position in the royal family, and eventually spawned a myriad of copycats (as well as a rereleased original)?

The iconic sheep sweater is baaaaa-ck (sorry, couldn't resist). Diana's original sheep sweater—first worn to a polo match the summer of 1981 before her marriage to Prince Charles—was knit by Warm & Wonderful, a London-based knitwear brand operating out of a stall in Covent Garden.

The sweater featured rows of white sheep and one black sheep, and the cheeky print became such a favorite of hers that she actually had another nearly identical one made, a discovery made by royal expert Elizabeth Holmes, author of *HRH: So Many Thoughts on Royal Style*. (The story was that her massive sapphire engagement ring snagged a thread on the inside of her first sweater.) She wore the next one in 1983, this time with a white blouse with black bow necktie. The sweater remained virtually the same, but the transformation from shy nineteen-year-old to international style icon was apparent.

The "black sheep jumper," an iconic Diana look and one that she would forever be associated with for its vibrant print and

PRINCESS DIANA   153

subtle "outsider" undertones, was relaunched by the original owners of Warm & Wonderful, Sally Muir and Joanna Osborne, in partnership with New York-based clothing brand Rowing Blazers in 2020.

Princess Diana was passionate about many causes during and after her royal tenure, including childrens' charities, helping the homeless, and the removal of land mines, but which one was she perhaps most famous for?

$\mathcal{J}$f there could be only one photo that summed up the Princess of Wales's enduring legacy, it is undoubtedly the image of Diana holding the hand of an AIDS patient in 1987—a time when the stigma of AIDS was so severe that many people believed the autoimmune disease could be transmitted through skin contact with a patient.

While most will immediately recognize the legendary snap, they may not know the full story behind the photograph. Diana, at age twenty-five, visited London Middlesex Hospital to open the Broderip Ward, UK's first dedicated unit to treating those with HIV/AIDS, according to the BBC. Two years earlier, half of the respondents of an *LA Times* poll felt people with AIDS should be quarantined, and in 1987, the US banned travelers with HIV from entering the country without a special waiver.

Nurses at the Broderip Ward even kept mum on the subject of which unit they worked in, for fear of association.

Only one patient, a man named Ivan Cohen, thirty-two, consented to have his photograph taken with Diana—but only from behind so that his face couldn't be identified in the newspapers. Her completely normal gesture of a handshake without wearing gloves sent shock waves around the world.

What infamous—and subsequently controversial—interview led Queen Elizabeth to urge Prince Charles and Princess Diana to expedite their divorce?

*D*iana's interview with journalist Martin Bashir for the BBC's *Panorama* was the final straw in a fraught marriage that broke down in front of a global audience. The "War of the Waleses" had reached a fever pitch. In the 1994 documentary *Charles: The Private Man, the Public Role*, the prince confirmed his affair with Camilla. When asked if he was faithful and honorable to Princess Diana during the marriage, he replied, "Yes. Until it became irretrievably broken down, us both having tried." After that, Diana sat for her own interview with Bashir.

The groundbreaking—and clandestine—interview took place in Kensington Palace on November 5, 1995, fifteen days before it aired on the BBC. Diana gave her staff the night off (it was Guy

Fawkes night) and let Martin Bashir (a relatively unknown journalist at the time) and a cameraman into her Kensington Palace apartments herself. Only a handful of people at the BBC even knew the sit-down was happening. The princess wore a black suit and heavy dark eyeliner, and answered difficult questions about her eating disorder, self-harm, her own affair, her doubts about Charles's ability to be the next king, her desire to be "a queen of people's hearts," and Charles's ongoing relationship with Camilla. "Well, there were three of us in this marriage, so it was a bit crowded." Diana famously told Bashir. No interview with a member of the royal family had ever been so candid—or explosive.

On December 20, Buckingham Palace announced the queen wrote to Charles and Diana and encouraged them to get a formal divorce, and the prime minister supported the decision. After fifteen years of marriage and four years of separation, in August 1996, Diana and Charles finalized their divorce.

Today, the interview is still making headlines for the dubious ways in which Bashir and the BBC secured the high-profile interview, then covered up the trail. In a report released by Lord Dyson in 2021, it was confirmed that Diana's brother Charles, 9th Earl Spencer, was shown falsified bank statements to convince him (and by extension, Diana) that palace courtiers were spying on Diana, which likely influenced her decision to participate. Prince William publicly denounced the interview based on these new revelations with a controversial statement that said: "It is my view that the deceitful way the interview was obtained substantially influenced what my mother said... It is my firm view that this *Panorama* program holds no legitimacy and should never be aired again."

It took several months for Princess Diana and Prince Charles to come to an agreement on the terms of their divorce. How come?

*N*early fifteen years since their fairy tale wedding at St. Paul's Cathedral, it was confirmed: As part of the divorce settlement in August 1996, Diana would receive a lump-sum payment (reported to have been approximately $22.5 million in cash and $600,000 a year to maintain her private office) versus regular alimony checks. (She reportedly asked for $75 million.)

Negotiating the finer points of their divorce is said to be the reason it took so long to sign on the dotted line. While the final statement from Buckingham Palace that the union was over said that the split was "amicable" and "greatly assisted by both the fairness of His Royal Highness the Prince of Wales's proposals and by Her Royal Highness the Princess of Wales's ready acceptance of them," that greatly glossed over the back and forth that ensued as Diana and Charles angrily worked to come to settle the proceedings. In fact, one of the biggest sticking points was Charles's insistence that Diana give up her right to be Queen of England and to be called "Her Royal Highness" despite the fact that Queen Elizabeth II was said to be okay with Diana retaining her HRH status. (Without the honorific, Diana would be obliged to curtsy to others who have it—not only Charles, but also her own kids.)

Speaking of William and Harry, Diana and Charles did agree to joint custody of the boys. Diana was also allowed to keep her apartment at Kensington Palace as well as access to the state apartments at St. James's Palace for entertaining as long as she asked permission first. The statement also read that Diana would always "be regarded as a member of the royal family" and would from time to time receive invitations to state and national occasions at the request of the sovereign or the government.

Of course, the bigger question at the time was about Diana's future role in the context of the monarchy. The palace kept things open-ended, saying that it would be "essentially for [Diana] to decide," but that she would have to clear any foreign trips (unless for private vacations) with the queen. And should Diana choose to remarry? Well, there was plenty of speculation that she'd likely have to relinquish much of what was drawn up in her divorce agreement, including her title Princess of Wales.

Princess Diana suffered from depression and what "secret disease" that, she said, became her "escape mechanism"?

*D*iana's battle with bulimia was brought into the spotlight once again with season four of *The Crown*, which provides a trigger warning for viewers before episodes that depict the princess's struggle with her eating disorder. Actress Emma Corrin portrays a young, lonely Diana in the throes of the disease, bingeing on food she raids from the royal kitchens late at night, then purging in the bathroom after.

Diana admitted she had struggled with the eating disorder to Martin Bashir during her BBC *Panorama* interview in 1995, telling him, "I had bulimia for a number of years. And that's like a secret disease. You inflict it upon yourself because your self-esteem is at a low ebb, and you don't think you're worthy or valuable. You fill your stomach up four or five times a day— some do it more—and it gives you a feeling of comfort. It's like having a pair of arms around you, but it's temporarily, temporary. Then you're disgusted at the bloatedness of your stomach, and then you bring it all up again."

She had also discussed her bulimia in the secret tapes she recorded for Andrew Morton's 1992 biography, *Diana: Her True Story*. "The bulimia started the week after we got engaged and would take nearly a decade to overcome," the princess was recorded saying. "My husband put his hand on my waistline and said: 'Oh, a bit chubby here, aren't we?' and that triggered off something in me—and the Camilla thing."

But the "secret disease" was also apparent before Diana's admissions, with tabloids running stories like "Darling Di, You're Lovely but Promise Us You Won't Lose One More Pound" (the *Sun*) next to a picture of a waifish-looking Princess Diana. Even Diana's wedding dress designer, Elizabeth Emanuel, later admitted that Diana had lost three inches off her waist from her fittings to her wedding day.

Princess Diana's "revenge dress"—an off-the-shoulder number, so nicknamed by the press because of its debut shortly after an interview aired where Charles admits to having an affair—was designed by who?

What to wear after your husband admits to cheating on you on national TV? A black off-the-shoulder, above-the-knee chiffon dress by Greek designer Christina Stambolian, that's what. In 1994, on the night *Charles: The Private Man, the Public Role* aired, Princess Diana attended a gala at the Serpentine Gallery dressed in a head-turning and form-fitting frock that later became known as her "revenge dress."

A last-minute outfit change actually led to the dress's dramatic debut. News of Prince Charles's guilty admission in the documentary broke two days before its actual airing, giving Diana enough time to prepare to knock the collective breath out of the public. Diana was originally planning to wear a long dress by Valentino, but the brand prematurely leaked her fashion decision to the press—a bit of a royal faux pas, since designers usually keep quiet about the royals' clothing until after they're seen sporting the fashions in public.

So the princess pulled a style switch, pairing her black Christina Stambolian dress with a pearl, sapphire, and diamond choker made from a brooch the Queen Mother gifted Diana as a wedding present, sheer black stockings, black stilettos, and red nail polish. Dress designer Stambolian later revealed in a Channel 4 documentary that the little black dress had been made three years prior for the princess, but Diana hadn't worn it back then because it was deemed "too daring."

After her separation from Prince Charles, Princess Diana took a few years' hiatus before getting back into the dating scene. Who was her first boyfriend after the separation?

While Diana and Charles's divorce wasn't finalized until August 1996, the couple had been officially separated since December 1992. After Charles rekindled his relationship with Camilla in 1986, Diana entered romantic relationships with Major James Hewitt (the family's former riding instructor) and Barry Mannakee (her former bodyguard). But her first long-term boyfriend post-separation was Dr. Hasnat Khan. (While Diana allegedly had an affair with married art dealer Oliver Hoare beginning in 1992, the reports were never proven.)

Diana struck up a two-year relationship with Pakistan-born Khan, a heart and lung surgeon, after the two met at the hospital Khan worked at in 1995. She reportedly visited his family in Lahore, Pakistan, in May 1996. Khan was described by Diana's former butler as her "soulmate" and "the true love of her life."

While Diana and Khan allegedly discussed marriage, the relationship soured when Khan realized he would never be able to have a normal family life under the harsh media scrutiny. "I told her that the only way I could see us having a vaguely normal life together would be if we went to Pakistan, as the press don't bother you there," Khan stated in the inquest into Diana's death. "I did not want to have to look over my shoulder all the time." Khan has remained remarkably tight-lipped about his relationship with Diana, vowing to never "cash in" on her when asked by the press in 2007 if he'd ever write a book about his time with the princess. Their relationship lasted two years, until the month of Diana's death in 1997, when she started dating Dodi Al Fayed.

In 1997, Princess Diana decided to auction off items from her wardrobe to benefit AIDS and cancer charities. Which clothing item garnered the highest bid—a whopping $222,500 (or over $360,000 in today's dollars)?

*W*hile Diana's collection of seventy-nine dresses fetched over $3.25 million at the Christie's auction, the biggest winner of the night was Princess Diana's ink-blue velvet "Travolta dress," nicknamed for the night she twirled around the dance floor with the actor at a White House reception in November 1985. The off-the-shoulder gown broke the previous Christie's record for a garment sale: $145,000. That item? The costume Travolta wore in *Saturday Night Fever*.

Princess Diana in the off-the-shoulder dress is the focal point of the iconic photo by former White House photographer Pete Souza, who reminisced on the evening in an Instagram caption posted in April 2021: "A few little-known facts from that night: Diana also danced that night with President Reagan, Tom Selleck, Clint Eastwood and Neil Diamond. She did not dance with Prince Charles. During her dance with John Travolta, the military band played a medley of songs from Travolta's movie, *Saturday Night Fever*."

John Travolta revealed to *Esquire México* in 2021 that it was a "fairy tale" he'd never forget. "Think of the setting. We were at the White House. It's midnight. The stage is like a dream. I approach her, touch her elbow, invite her to dance," he said. "She spins around and gives me that captivating smile, just a little sad, and accepts my invitation. And there we were, dancing together as if it were a fairy tale." He also said he knew the princess enjoyed the moment just as much as he did. "I'm so honored that I was able to experience this, and I know for a fact that it was her highlight of being in the United States; it was her favorite moment," he said.

Other dresses that sold at the Christie's Auction: a pearl-covered column dress Diana herself referred to as her "Elvis dress," a white Catherine Walker beaded halter cocktail dress, and her Christian Stambolian "revenge dress." And who does she have to thank for the selection? Reportedly, it was Prince William who helped his "mummy" clean out her closet, instructing her about the pieces she should put up for auction and which ones looked too worn to sell.

Diana didn't actually attend the auction in New York City (she instead attended a pre-auction event in New York before returning to London), but she did request a fax of the auction results be sent overnight and delivered on her breakfast tray at Kensington Palace the next morning.

Princess Diana was tragically killed in a car crash in Paris. Who was she with and what was the cause of the accident?

$\mathcal{P}$rincess Diana was declared dead in Paris, France, after a lethal car accident on August 31, 1997. She died at age thirty-six (just over one year since her divorce was finalized). Diana and boyfriend Dodi Al Fayed and driver Henri Paul all died from the accident. There was a fourth passenger, Diana's bodyguard, who was seriously injured but survived.

Diana and Dodi had been vacationing in the French Riviera and arrived in Paris the previous day. (Quick refresher: they had only known each other around forty days when this all happened, though they'd run into each other at events in the years leading up to this.) That night, they left the Ritz Paris, intending to go to Dodi's apartment. Immediately upon leaving the hotel, a swarm of paparazzi on motorcycles began aggressively tailing their car. About three minutes later, the driver lost control and crashed into a pillar at the entrance of the Pont de l'Alma tunnel, reportedly reaching a speed of almost 70 mph (the posted speed limit was 50 km/h, or 30 mph).

One of the first responders to the crash described the horrific scene: "The car was in a mess and we just dealt with it like any road accident. I held her hand and told her to be calm and keep still; I said I was there to help and reassured her." During an inquest, it was revealed that Diana's bodyguard kept repeating "Where is she? Where is she?" He later was in a ten-day coma for facial reconstruction surgery, but he maintains he doesn't remember much from the evening (he reportedly suffered severe head trauma). However, her bodyguard did say he could hear a woman's voice (probably Diana's) moaning and uttering Dodi's name. Dodi and the driver were pronounced dead on the scene, but Diana was taken to the hospital and was pronounced dead at 6:00 a.m.

Her coffin was flown via helicopter back to London from Paris on August 31, 1997, accompanied by Prince Charles and Diana's two sisters. Her funeral took place on September 6, 1997.

Princess Diana was buried with a set of rosary beads, gifted to her by what famous religious figure?

Diana's funeral was attended by royals, foreign dignitaries, celebrities, diplomats, and charity representatives, but perhaps the most religious contribution came by way of Mother Teresa, who had gifted the princess a set of rosary beads and who died the day before Diana's funeral.

The Princess of Wales was laid to rest with the rosary beads and a photo of Princes William and Harry in her hands, along with a Spencer family flag draped over her coffin. The picture of her sons was found in her handbag the night she died, and was one she always traveled with, according to Andrew Morton's biography, *Diana: Her True Story*.

The royal standard with an ermine border, also known as "the Other Members' Standard" was draped over her casket for the funeral procession. On top, three white wreaths (one from her brother, Charles, 9th Earl Spencer, and one from each of her sons) plus a note from Prince Harry that was addressed to "Mummy" were arranged. When it came time to bury Diana, "the Other Members' Standard" was replaced with a Spencer family flag, which caused some to believe that it was Diana's brother's way of dissing the royal family.

Diana's former butler, Paul *Burrell*, told the press that Charles Spencer even said, "She is a Spencer now," when they buried her. Diana's brother later rebuked the media reports and released a statement saying "The Queen's standard was removed as part of the ceremony by her own officer in a dignified and pre-agreed manner." That said, he didn't hold back when eulogizing his sister, reportedly angering the queen when he said, "Someone with a natural nobility who was classless and who proved in the last year that she needed no royal title to continue to generate her particular brand of magic..." and "I pledge that we, your blood family, will do all we can to continue the imaginative and loving way in which you were steering these two exceptional young men so that their souls are not simply immersed by duty and tradition, but can sing openly as you planned."

The princess's final resting place is Althorp, the Spencer family estate. She is buried on a secluded island in the middle of an ornamental lake called the Round Oval. A path with thirty-six oak trees, marking each year of her life, leads to the lake. On the southern edge of the Round Oval sits Diana's memorial, housed in a former summer house that was moved from London to the Spencer gardens in 1901.

Diana's name is carved into the stone of the memorial. A black bench sits beneath a black marble silhouette of the princess. Hanging next to it is a quote from Diana inscribed in marble. The quote reads, "Nothing brings me more happiness than trying to help the most vulnerable people in society—it is a goal and an essential part of my life, a kind of destiny—and whoever is in distress can call on me. I will come running wherever they are."

On the other side, a quote from her brother's eulogy at Westminster reads, "We give thanks for the life of a woman I am so proud to call my sister: the unique, the complex, the extraordinary and irreplaceable Diana, whose beauty both internal and external will never be extinguished from our minds."

PART IV

PRINCE CHARLES

Prince Charles, the eldest son of then Princess Elizabeth, was born on November 14, 1948. His arrival marked a change in royal protocol. What was it?

*A*head of Prince Charles Philip Arthur George's arrival in the Buhl Room—which had been converted into a mini hospital—at Buckingham Palace, his mother was said to have been in labor for thirty hours before finally delivering her firstborn son (and future heir to the throne) via Cesarean section. But Elizabeth's father, King George VI, allowed Elizabeth, who was just twenty-two at the time, to break with royal tradition for the delivery and waived the requirement that a senior politician (say, the prime minister or home secretary) be there to witness and verify the royal birth. Instead, Elizabeth gave birth on her own—with an assist from the royal surgeon and gynecologist Sir William Gilliatt. In fact, Prince Philip, the Duke of Edinburgh, also wasn't there to see the arrival of his son. He was playing squash with his private secretary and brought Elizabeth a bouquet of red roses and carnations upon hearing the news. (Prince Philip was only present for the birth of the queen's fourth child, Prince Edward, but that was the norm at the time.)

A BBC Home Service news bulletin also announced Charles's arrival and the fact that Princess Elizabeth was "safely delivered of a prince." Philip's reaction at the time was that Charles resembled "a plum pudding." His debut was greeted with a forty-one-gun salute fired off by the King's Troop Royal Horse Artillery, and the bells of Westminster Abbey rang out in celebration of the happy news. Shortly after, on December 15, Charles was christened in the Music Room of Buckingham Palace. (At the time, royal christenings were typically held in the palace's chapel, but it had been so badly damaged during World War II, they had to find a work-around.)

Charles's sister, Princess Anne, arrived soon after, on August 15, 1950. (There was a gap between Prince Andrew and Prince Edward, who were born on February 19, 1960, and March 10, 1964, respectively.)

What event led to Prince Charles being named the heir apparent when he was just three years old?

On February 6, 1952, Princess Elizabeth's father—and Charles's grandfather—King George VI passed away peacefully in his sleep at Sandringham. It was this event that elevated Queen Elizabeth II to the throne and placed Charles as the heir apparent at the young age of three.

Four months prior, the king had undergone an operation to remove a growth on his right lung, but his health had been deteriorating for quite some time. He was just fifty-seven years old, but entering the sixteenth year of his reign—something he never quite desired to do, but was forced into when his brother Edward VIII abdicated to marry Wallis Simpson. Still, King George had been expected to recover from the operation and had been out shooting just a day before his death. He'd also been present at London (now Heathrow) Airport that same week to wave his daughter off as she left for what was to be a tour of East Africa, Australia, and New Zealand.

Instead, Elizabeth was called back, and sixteen months later, on June 2, 1953, was crowned Queen Elizabeth II at Westminster Abbey. (See Part V, "The Queen," about the gap between the king's death and Elizabeth's coronation.) By that point, Charles was four years old, and his mother did everything she could to make her coronation feel kid-friendly (when it was anything but). She had an invitation to the event specially hand-painted for the young prince featuring British guards playing instruments and a cartoon lion and unicorn, both symbols on Queen Elizabeth's royal coat of arms. Still, photos from the occasion show Charles looking quite bored, sandwiched between the Queen Mother and Princess Margaret during the coronation ceremony.

Gasp! He also almost dropped the Imperial State Crown. Lady Anne Glenconner was one of the queen's attendants on the day and recently shared on the podcast *My Life in Seven Charms* that when the queen took it off, Charles made a beeline for it. "We thought he was going to drop it," she said. "We thought, 'Oh my goodness, that would be a bad omen.' But luckily, I think my mother, as a lady-in-waiting, seized it from him and took it away."

As of 2021, Charles is still the longest-serving British heir to the throne: at seventy-two years old, he's been in that position for nearly seventy years.

Prince Charles spent much of his early life and upbringing apart from his parents, a lot due to his father's role in the Royal Navy and Elizabeth's commitments as princess, then queen. Whom did he spend time with instead?

With Prince Philip stationed all over the world due to his role as an officer in the Royal Navy, it was a priority for Queen Elizabeth II to spend as much time with Philip as she could. When Philip was posted to Malta in winter of 1949, the queen departed to be with him, leaving Charles, who had only just turned one, on his own for five months. Of course, he wasn't completely by himself. He had his nannies looking after him, but the little prince found a great deal of happiness in the relationship he shared with his grandmother, the Queen Mother.

She was based at Royal Lodge in Windsor Great Park (where Prince Andrew and his ex-wife Sarah Ferguson, Duchess of York, now live), and Charles tended to visit her there anytime his parents were away. According to reports, she not only gave Charles the hugs he craved—a marked contrast to the handshake greeting offered to him by his parents when he was just five and they'd been away from him for nearly six months—but also is the one who helped him develop a love and appreciation for both music and art. As Charles himself once described it, "My grandmother was the person who taught me to look at things."

While his own parents worried about his sensitive and gentle nature, Charles's grandmother championed it. At the time, Charles struggled quite a bit with his distant relationships with his parents and had a hard time finding common ground with his father. As his biographer, Jonathan Dimbleby, wrote in 1994, Charles considered many of his father's actions to be bullying and belittling during his formative years. As for his mother the queen, he famously described her as "not indifferent so much as detached."

Prince Charles was the first heir to be educated outside Buckingham Palace. Where did he attend school?

*A*lthough Charles began his education with homeschooling, his mother, Queen Elizabeth II, and Prince Philip soon made the decision to send him to actual school where he could be around other kids. While he was originally sent to Hill House School in Knightsbridge in 1957 (he was almost nine), six months later he was moved to Cheam School in Hampshire, a school Prince Philip had attended as a young boy and said to be the oldest private school in the country. (It was founded in 1645; Charles was a student there up through age thirteen.)

Cheam was more progressive than other private schools of its kind, and Charles had a hard time fitting in. He wasn't athletic and preferred his own company to that of groups. As a result, he endured ridicule from his classmates and extreme homesickness. (He wrote to his parents weekly to share his unhappiness.) The queen even acknowledged Charles's inability to fit in in a letter she sent to Prime Minister Anthony Eden in early 1958: "Charles is just beginning to dread the return to school next week—so much worse for the second term."

Still, Cheam is the place where Charles is said to have first realized the gravity of the fact that he was, indeed, heir to the throne. During the closing ceremony of 1958 British Empire and Commonwealth Games in Cardiff, Wales, he was watching the televised broadcast with some classmates. In a pre-recorded speech aired during the ceremony, he heard his mother announce that she would be naming Charles the Prince of Wales.

A pivotal moment in Prince Charles's early life was Prince Philip's decision to send him to Gordonstoun in Scotland, an education that he viewed as a "prison sentence." What made his time there so bad?

*D*espite encouragement from the Queen Mother to send Charles to Eton College after Cheam, Prince Philip won out when it came to Charles's continued education, and the Prince of Wales was shipped off to Gordonstoun in Scotland, the same place Philip had studied as a kid. But for Charles's timid temperament, the school couldn't have been a more terrible fit.

In May 1962, Philip delivered Charles to school himself, where he was assigned to one of seven residences—formerly used as Royal Air Force barracks—along with thirteen other boys. The school prioritized instilling both intellect and character, the latter of which was taught through a variety of physical challenges, ranging from pre-breakfast runs followed by cold showers (even in the winter) to dormitory windows left open at all times (again, regardless of the season). Founder Kurt Hahn's objective was to create an egalitarian society where privilege had no bearing on your circumstance. Philip flourished in this environment, but Charles shrank. Unlike his father, he wasn't athletic, nor did he have anonymity, given his position as heir to the throne. As a result, he was bullied from day one.

One housemaster in particular—Robert Whitby—empowered senior boys in charge of running the residences to impose a form of martial law, which resulted in merciless psychological and physical abuse. Charles was taunted relentlessly by his peers for things ranging from a physical attribute like his ears, but also just for being who he was (*ahem*, the future king). The result was very few friends on campus aside from his bodyguard, Donald Green, who—much to Charles's chagrin—was let go from his position after a fourteen-year-old Charles was caught ordering a cherry brandy by a tabloid reporter. (As the story goes, he was taken to a pub during his second year and ordered the first alcoholic beverage that popped into his head.) His underage drinking made international headlines and, alas, Green was fired, leaving Charles feeling more alone than ever.

During a gap year from Gordonstoun, Prince Charles left Europe for the first time in his life. Where did he study?

*I*t was Prince Philip's decision to send Charles to Australia for two terms when he was seventeen years old and nearing his final year at Gordonstoun. He attended Timbertop in Melbourne, part of the Geelong Grammar School, which was less focused on academics and more on a robust outdoor education. Charles arrived in February 1966 and, much to his own surprise, fell in love with the locale, mainly due to the fact that there wasn't a lot of attention placed on who he was. There was no hazing—and also very little homesickness. Instead, Charles embraced the physicality required of the experience, enjoying cross-country expeditions with his classmates and camping out in freezing-cold temps under the stars. Most importantly, Charles's time in Australia gave him the chance to prove to his dad that he was, in fact, physically capable.

Under the supervision of Prince Philip's low-key equerry David Checketts, Charles was also able to kick back and relax. He spent weekends with the Checketts family, going fishing, playing with their kids, and finally found a chance to let his guard down. While he was only in Australia for six months, Charles loved it, mainly due to the fact that it was the polar opposite of Gordonstoun. It was also the place where he first began to grow into his public role. In Australia, he took on nearly fifty official engagements on behalf of the Crown, handling each one with confidence and prowess. At the time, Australians welcomed Charles with open arms.

During his schooling, Prince Charles was the first royal heir to earn a bachelor's degree, studying archaeology and history at Trinity College. But before he graduated in 1970, he spent a single term coming up to speed on a subject critical to his royal title. What was it?

Cue one of the most poignant episodes of season three of *The Crown*: Prince Charles takes a semester off from his schooling at Trinity College, Cambridge, to brush up on his Welsh at Aberystwyth University ahead of his investiture as Prince of Wales. Prime Minister Harold Wilson encouraged it, and so the decision was made: Send Charles to Wales. Welsh nationalism was on the rise—along with a push for more public recognition of the Welsh language—and Wilson thought it would be smart for Charles to prioritize his study of it, given the mounting anger that yet another English-born man would be named the Prince of Wales. (Queen Elizabeth II agreed with his recommendation.)

Upon arrival, Charles was met with protestors (he later told the *Telegraph*, "Every day I had to go down to the town where I went to these lectures, and most days there seemed to be a demonstration going on against me"), then placed under the tutelage of Dr. Edward "Tedi" Millward, who just so happened to also be vice president of Plaid Cymru, a political party advocating for Welsh independence. (Millward was also deeply against the monarchy in general.) In fact, Millward himself dismissed Charles at the start, deeming his interest in the Welsh language and culture purely for optics. But it didn't take long for Charles to prove him wrong.

Millward (who passed away in 2020) spoke to the *Guardian* about the experience: "The early '60s was the start of an upsurge in Welsh nationalism that saw the first Plaid Cymru politician elected to Parliament... By that point, I was a well-known nationalist, so I was a little surprised when the university asked me if I would teach Welsh to Prince Charles, for a term, in 1969... He had a one-on-one tutorial with me once a week. He was eager, and did a lot of talking. By the end, his accent was quite good. Toward the end of his term, he said good morning—'Bore da'—to a woman at college; she turned to him and said: 'I don't speak Welsh!'"

During his schooling, Prince Charles excelled at some subjects—art and music, for example—and struggled with others like sports and math. But the discovery of what interest was something that led him to a lifelong passion?

*I*t's true: Cheam wasn't Charles's favorite place to be. But there was one positive to come out of it for the future Prince of Wales. During his time there, Charles discovered his love of theater. Cast as King Richard III in a play called *The Last Baron*, Charles is said to have come alive, performing the part in front of an audience that included both the Queen Mother and Princess Anne. The Queen Mother even remarked in a letter to her daughter, Queen Elizabeth II: "After a few minutes, on to the stage shambled a most horrible-looking creature—a leering vulgarian, with a dreadful expression on his twisted mouth. To my horror, I began to realize that this was my dear grandson!" (She did add that he performed quite well in the role.)

Whereas Charles wasn't naturally prone to things like rugby or horseback riding (his sister Princess Anne competed in the 1976 Olympics due to her skill), theater became a lifelong outlet and interest for the prince. At Gordonstoun, he played Macbeth in the Shakespearean drama of the same name; after enrolling at Trinity College, Cambridge, in 1967, Charles found his way into the school's theater troupe, called the Dryden Society. As part of that, he participated in student sketches and revues, playing everything from a weather forecaster to a sports commentator to an antiques expert. He even wrote some of his own material.

The Prince of Wales didn't stop there. Charles is also said to have had a strong interest in magic. In 1975, he was inducted into the Magic Circle, which touts itself as the world's premiere magic society, after he performed a classic disappearing trick with cups and a ball to earn his membership. In fact, it was Charles's uncle Lord Mountbatten who first introduced Charles to the art. (Mountbatten had been a member of the Magic Circle for two decades before Charles was invited in.)

When Prince Charles was born, he wasn't automatically the Prince of Wales. At what age was he formally presented with that title?

Charles—who has been Prince of Wales for more than half a century—was officially given the title in 1958 via letters patent (a written order issued by the queen), but he had to wait until July 1, 1969, when he was twenty years old, for his formal investiture ceremony (aka the moment when he was presented to the Welsh people as their prince). It was held at Caernarfon Castle in Wales, and fresh off his study of the Welsh language with Dr. Edward "Tedi" Millward, Charles was more than ready to assume his new role.

There were four thousand people present (and five hundred million people tuned in around the world) to watch Queen Elizabeth II give Charles the traditional symbols that signify his role as Prince of Wales, including the sword, coronet, ring, gold rod, and kingly mantle. Charles also took an oath before delivering a speech in both English and Welsh, one that was well received by the crowd, but also considered controversial for the subtle boost it was thought to give Welsh nationalism, according to Cabinet papers that were later released. Charles later said of the experience: "For me, by far the most moving and meaningful moment came when I put my hands between Mummy's and swore to be liege man of life and limb and to live and die against all manner of folks—such magnificent, medieval, appropriate words, even if they were never adhered to in those old days."

Something else that was unique about Charles's investiture: It was planned by the Earl of Snowdon (Princess Margaret's husband), given his photography experience. At the end of the '60s, there was a real push to make events of this kind television-friendly in order to give the world more access to the pomp and circumstance of royal life. There was also heightened security with over 250 extra police officers deployed after a homemade bomb detonated and killed its makers on the eve of the occasion.

To this day, Charles speaks Welsh to the best of his ability whenever he is in Wales. He also has assumed quite a few other titles in addition to Prince of Wales, the Duke of Cornwall included.

Fresh off his career as a member of the Royal Navy, what philanthropic organization did Prince Charles use his military severance pay to launch?

Charles spent six months undergoing aviation training with the Royal Air Force before officially joining the Royal Navy in 1971 and serving aboard the HMS *Norfolk* and two frigates. In 1973, he was promoted to acting lieutenant and, in 1974, he served as a helicopter pilot for the 845 Naval Air Squadron, which was based aboard the HMS *Hermes*. Charles's active military service concluded in 1976 aboard the HMS *Bronington*, where he served as commander.

Upon his exit and using his navy severance pay—£7,400—he set up the Prince's Trust, an organization designed to fund a number of community initiatives that would help improve the lives of disadvantaged youth in the UK. At the time, the UK was facing the major problem of massive youth unemployment.

The Prince's Trust focused on combating it, starting with twenty-one pilot projects, each designed to make an impact—from providing funds for a nineteen-year-old woman to run a social center to helping two ex-offenders set up a fishing club. Charles recently described his decision to launch in a piece he penned for the *Telegraph*: "It seemed to me that we should do something to make a difference, however small... That was how the Prince's Trust began: initially with the aid of my severance pay from the navy, and later with the help of innumerable donations in cash and in kind from people and institutions from every possible walk of life..."

As of 2021, the Prince's Trust has been in existence for nearly forty-six years. It also launched a US chapter that same year.

One of the most pivotal moments of Prince Charles's life was said to occur when his uncle, Lord Mountbatten, was killed. What was their relationship really like?

Lord Louis Mountbatten—1st Earl Mountbatten of Burma, the last viceroy of India, and the first sea lord of the British Navy—made quite the impact on an impressionable Charles. To him, he was just Uncle Dickie (Prince Philip's uncle) and a man who was frequently put in the position of mentoring Charles as he charted his course as Prince of Wales. After all, it was

Dickie who recommended Charles go to Trinity and join the Royal Navy; Dickie who accompanied Charles on his first trip to Wales after his investiture; Dickie who encouraged Charles to play the field, then find a "suitable, attractive and sweet-charactered girl" to settle down with, according to a letter he penned to Charles in 1974. Bottom line: the pair were close.

That's why, in August 1979, Charles was gutted when a bomb planted by the Irish Republican Army aboard Lord Mountbatten's fishing boat in Donegal Bay off the coast of Ireland went off, killing not only Mountbatten, but three others—his fourteen-year-old grandson included. Charles spoke emphatically about his uncle's legacy at his funeral at St. Paul's Cathedral, saying: "That quality of real moral courage, of being able to face unpleasant tasks that needed to be done—and yet to be fair and consistent—is a rare quality indeed. But he had it in abundance and that, I think, is one of the reasons why people would have followed him into hell, if he had explained the point of such an expedition. It is also one of the reasons why I adored him and why so many of us miss him so dreadfully now."

Charles's vulnerability after the loss of his uncle is also said to have led him into the arms of Diana. According to Andrew Morton's *Diana: Her True Story*, the pair reunited a year after the funeral in 1980 and Diana reportedly told Charles: "You looked so sad when you walked up the aisle at Mountbatten's funeral. It was the most tragic thing I've ever seen. My heart bled for you when I watched. I thought, 'You're so lonely—you should be with somebody to look after you.'" Per Diana, Charles leapt on her after that.

In between his relationship with Camilla and before becoming engaged to Diana in 1980, Prince Charles actually played the field quite a bit. Who did he date?

*I*t's true: Lord Mountbatten once encouraged Charles to "sow his wild oats" before settling down. Apparently, Charles did, dating close to twenty different women between the years of 1967 and 1980 before deciding Diana was the one. Included in those relationships? One of Charles's early romances with Lucia Santa Cruz, daughter of the former Chilean ambassador to London. The pair were introduced by a mutual friend at a dinner party in 1967, but Lucia is also the woman who first introduced the Prince of Wales to Camilla. Per Jonathan Dimbleby's authorized biography, titled *The Prince of Wales: A Biography*, Lucia even arranged their first meeting, saying she had "just the girl" for Charles.

Of course, Camilla entered the picture next, but only for a brief period of time in 1970. A smitten Charles dated her for approximately six months before he left to serve in the Royal Navy for eight months, at which point Camilla got engaged to her boyfriend Andrew Parker Bowles. (Camilla and Andrew married in 1973.)

Charles was devastated, but back on the market. This led to relationships with Lady Jane Wellesley (daughter of the 8th Duke of Wellington), Sabrina Guinness, heiress to the brewing dynasty, and, of course, rather famously, Lady Sarah Spencer. Charles retreated after that.

Still, when the clock struck 1978 and Charles hit his self-imposed marriage deadline of thirty, the pressure on the royal heir began to mount. Lord Mountbatten—who had introduced Queen Elizabeth and Prince Philip—attempted to play matchmaker once again, introducing Charles to his granddaughter Amanda Knatchbull, who was nine years Charles's junior. The pair dated seriously for a stint, but when Charles proposed marriage in 1979, she turned him down, saying she had no interest in the media spotlight that would be attached to the marriage.

It wasn't long after that Charles reconnected with Lady Diana Spencer, the woman who would become Princess of Wales.

It was the wedding of the century on July 29, 1981, when Prince Charles married Princess Diana at St. Paul's Cathedral. But his proposal to Diana was one made under pressure. How come?

*W*as it ill-fated from the start? A young Prince Charles always knew he had to find a suitable wife to be his bride (and mother to the future heir), one who was aristocratic or had noble blood, had a "pure" reputation, and wasn't Catholic (a legal requirement that was changed in 2013).

Camilla didn't fit the bill. Charles was still enjoying the bachelor life when they first met, she wasn't from an aristocratic family, and she had a certain reputation that his uncle, Lord Mountbatten, had warned against. Besides, at that point, Camilla was spoken for. On February 6, 1981, after just thirteen dates and six months of courtship, Charles proposed to Lady Diana Spencer.

But what convinced him to pop the question? For one, Charles felt pressured by his father, Prince Philip. He revealed as much in his authorized biography written by British journalist Jonathan Dimbloby. Dimbloby wrote that Prince Philip had given his son an ultimatum to marry Diana, saying she would otherwise be compromised after news got out that she had visited Charles at Balmoral, the Queen's Scottish castle.

Philip argued Diana had "no past" and was young enough to be molded into the future queen. "The prince, in a state of emotional confusion, clung to these calculations," wrote Dimbleby. "The pressures on him began to sweep him toward his destiny."

According to biographer Penny Junor, in private letters to a friend, Charles wrote, "Because I do very much want to do the right thing for this country and for my family—but I'm terrified sometimes of making a promise and then perhaps living to regret it. It is just a matter of taking an unusual plunge into some rather unknown circumstances that inevitably disturbs me but I expect it will be the right thing in the end."

During their honeymoon, Prince Charles wore a pair of cuff links that Princess Diana would later credit with the beginning of their marital troubles. What did the engraving say?

*A*fter the "wedding of the century," newlyweds Princess Diana and Prince Charles set off for their honeymoon: a fourteen-day cruise aboard the Royal Yacht *Britannia* after a stay at an English country estate in Hampshire. Sailing from Gibraltar, Spain, the two were supposed to celebrate their marriage while taking in the sights of the Mediterranean and Aegean Sea. They visited the Algerian Coast, the Greek isles (including a stop on Ithaca), and Cairo, Egypt, then ended their honeymoon at a hunting lodge near Balmoral Castle in Scotland, where Diana's new in-laws were currently staying.

At dinner one night with the Egyptian president, the Prince of Wales donned a pair of silver cuff links featuring two entwined Cs—one for Charles and one for his former flame, Camilla Parker Bowles. A gift from an old lover? Diana was furious. (See Part III, "Princess Diana," for more about the cuff links.)

Diana's former butler Paul Burrell said in the 2019 documentary *The Royal Family* that the design of the two Cs haunted Diana throughout her failing marriage. "She made me pick off all the Cs off her Chanel shoes and the Chanel handbags because she couldn't bear to see two Cs entwined," he said.

Charles reportedly also phoned Camilla every day while on board the yacht, according to Charles's valet, Stephen Barry, in *The Diana Chronicles* by biographer Tina Brown.

Prince Charles and Princess Diana were on a skiing trip in Switzerland that many credit with having a profound impact on Charles's life and outlook. What happened?

*I*n 1988, in the midst of marital troubles and a few years before their separation, Diana and Charles experienced a tragic accident that many say deeply affected the Prince of Wales for years to come. While on one of their regular holidays to the swanky Swiss ski resort Klosters, an avalanche killed one of their companions, Major Hugh Lindsay, and badly injured another. The accident was explored in *The Crown* season four, in the episode titled "Avalanche."

Princess Diana and Sarah Ferguson, who married Prince Andrew two years prior and was pregnant with Princess Beatrice at the time, decided to skip the outing—and it may have saved their lives. Charles, Major Lindsay (a close friend of Charles and Diana's and a former aide to the queen), Patricia Palmer-Tomkinson, and three other skiers, including a guide, were standing on Gotschnagrat Mountain when the avalanche started.

Though Prince Charles was skiing that day, he miraculously wasn't caught in the onslaught of snow that began tumbling down the steep slope of "the Wang," a notoriously dangerous ski run. Major Lindsay and Palmer-Tomkinson were buried in the show. Charles and the rest of the party began to dig them out once the snow stopped cascading, according to a 1988 article from the *Guardian*. Eyewitnesses said that Prince Charles, who was lifted off the slope by a second helicopter, was visibly distressed. The second helicopter pilot was quoted by local journalists as saying the prince was weeping.

Major Lindsay was pronounced dead after being airlifted to a nearby hospital, but Palmer-Tomkinson survived (though she suffered two broken legs, a collapsed lung, and underwent multiple surgeries). Charles and Diana left Klosters shortly after the accident and attended Major Lindsay's funeral a week later, alongside Fergie, Prince Andrew, and the queen. Major Lindsay's wife Sarah was pregnant at the time and worked in the Buckingham Palace press office. The couple had been married only eight months.

Could it have been prevented? An avalanche warning had reportedly been issued that day, and the group had willingly followed Charles, an avid skier, down a challenging, unmarked slope. According to the *Los Angeles Times*, an investigation in June of the same year found that Charles was cleared of any personal fault during the criminal inquiry, but that the entire group was responsible for not heeding the warning.

Diana discussed the accident in the secret tapes she recorded for Andrew Morton's *Diana: Her True Story*. "Fergie and I were closer to Hugh than Charles ever was. Hugh just felt sorry for Charles. He was very good with all the members of my husband's family, he was always a star trooper," Diana said.

Diana also provided details about the aftermath of the avalanche. "We arrived back at Northolt and we had Hugh's coffin in the bottom of the aeroplane and Sarah [Lindsay's wife] was waiting at Northolt, six months pregnant and it was a ghastly sight, just chilling. The whole thing was ghastly, and what a nice person he was. Out of all the people who went it should never have been him."

In the early '90s, Prince Charles was hard at work building back his reputation after the very public separation from Princess Diana. Then, he landed in hot water. Why?

*U*p until the summer of '94, Prince Charles had been on a PR campaign for himself, working to bolster his public image during what was dubbed by the press as "the War of the Waleses." It had been Princess Diana's word—through the Andrew Morton biography—against his.

But in *Charles: The Private Man, the Public Role*, the otherwise sympathetic 2.5-hour ITV documentary about the prince's life meant to mark the twenty-fifth anniversary of his investiture as the Prince of Wales, Charles came clean about his affair with Camilla Parker Bowles. Jonathan Dimbleby, who conducted the interview in the doc, asked Charles if he had been "faithful and honorable" when he married Lady Diana in July 1981.

"Yes, absolutely," Charles replied. "And you were?" pressed Dimbleby. "Yes," Prince Charles repeated. Then, after a slight pause, he added, "Until it became irretrievably broken down, us both having tried." At another point in the film, Charles referred to Camilla as a "great friend" and that there was "no truth" to the speculation and tabloid reports about his private life. (It's worth noting that this doc aired the year after a phone conversation—dubbed "Camillagate" by the press—leaked and confirmed the intimacy between Charles and Camilla and caused a huge scandal for the royal family.)

The British tabloids had a field day, even before the documentary aired on national television. (It was screened to the press days before it aired.) The headlines read, "Charles: I Cheated on Diana" and "Di Told You So." Stateside, the *New York Times* ran, "Prince Charles, in TV Documentary, Admits to Infidelity." A short time later, in August 1996, Charles finalized his divorce from Diana; Camilla divorced her first husband Andrew in January 1995.

Some unforeseen developments resulted in Prince Charles and Camilla's long-awaited wedding getting pushed one day and moved to a different location. What were they?

What's a wedding without a few last-minute changes? Unfortunately for Charles and Camilla, those changes were anything but minor: the couple not only had to move their wedding date twenty-four hours forward, but they also had to change the location.

In order to attend Pope John Paul II's funeral on behalf of his mother the queen, Prince Charles had to move his wedding date from April 8 to April 9, 2005. The move also meant that many of the foreign heads of state who were attending the funeral were also able to make it to the Prince of Wales's wedding the next day. But what about the commemorative coffee mugs and tea towels already printed with the now incorrect date? Manufacturers had to quickly update their designs, though the items with the original "April 8" date actually became a hot collectors' item for a short time.

The couple also had to move the location of their legal wedding from Windsor Castle to Windsor Guildhall, which is located directly outside the gates to the castle. Because Charles and Camilla were both divorced, they needed to have a civil marriage ceremony—a royal family first. However, this meant that if they were to have a civil ceremony within Windsor Castle's St. George's Chapel, because of some legal requirements, they'd need to open up the option to other couples looking to get hitched in a civil ceremony for at least the next three years. Instead, they just decided to move the wedding.

After their civil wedding, which was attended by senior members of the royal family except for the queen and Prince

Philip, the couple had a royal blessing ceremony at St. George's Chapel. This part of their wedding saw some eight hundred guests, including the queen and Prince Philip, attend.

Prince Charles's official London residence was previously occupied by the Queen Mother. It's also the name of Prince Charles and the Duchess of Cornwall's offices and team. What is it?

Welcome to Clarence House! Not only is Clarence House the couple's official royal residence and office name, it's also the name of Charles and Camilla's shared social media accounts. Charles and Camilla's other residences outside of London are Highgrove House in Gloucestershire, Birkhall in Scotland, and Llwynywermod in Wales.

The four-story house is one of the last remaining aristocratic townhouses in London, though it's undergone extensive renovations since World War II. It's attached to St. James's Palace, located in Pall Mall, and shares the gardens of the palace. Prince Charles uses the gardens to grow squash, peppers, tomatoes, and kumquats.

For six years, Clarence House was the home of his mother and father, then Princess Elizabeth and Prince Philip, after their wedding and before she ascended the throne. Elizabeth was said to be very fond of the home, which is much more pared back than the expansive and richly decorated Buckingham Palace—and felt more like a family home to the young queen. In fact, Sir Winston Churchill reportedly had to strongly persuade the queen and Philip to make the switch to Buckingham Palace after her father died. Tears were shed, according to Penny Junor in her 2005 biography *The Firm*.

Then, for nearly fifty years after that, it was occupied by Queen Elizabeth the Queen Mother until 2002. After the Queen Mother's death and extensive renovations to update the furnishings, Charles, Camilla, and then-teenaged William and Harry moved in. Princes William and Harry's rooms on the top floor were more modern in decoration, while the rest of the house has elements that honor the Queen Mother, like a portrait of her with one of her corgis hanging in the Morning Room.

The house (the ground floor at least) is typically open for public tours in August, when Charles and Camilla go to Birkhall in Scotland. If you're there, you may spot a few of Charles's very own watercolor paintings that adorn the Cornwall Room.

Prince Charles's philanthropic work has focused largely on climate change, the environment, and sustainability, but he also incorporates the causes into his day-to-day life. For example, he keeps 150,000 bees at his home at Highgrove. Also, Charles's car runs on the byproduct of what common aperitif?

*W*e know the royals lead pretty lavish lives, but the idea that Prince Charles owns a car that (kind of) runs on excess white wine? It's true. In 2008, Charles wanted to convert his Aston Martin Volante, a car he's driven since he was twenty-one, to run on alternative fuel sources. Engineers thought they could make it happen with a biofuel made from white wine.

"They discovered they could run it on surplus English white wine, but also I hadn't realized that they had mixed whey into it, too," the Prince of Wales said in the BBC documentary *Prince, Son and Heir: Charles at 70*. He convinced them to press on with their experiment, even though there were problems along the way. "The engineers at Aston said, 'Oh, it'll ruin the whole thing.' And I said, 'Well, I won't drive it, then,' so they got on with it and now they admit that it runs better and is more powerful on that fuel than it is on petrol."

The engineers figured out how to make it happen by creating a biofuel made from a mixture of bioethanol and regular gas, or petrol. The bioethanol is derived from a vast number of sources of waste biomass, one of them being surplus wine. "Also, it smells delicious as you're driving along," Charles added.

Charles has led the charge to scale back the royal family's reliance on fossil fuels in other ways as well. He instigated the royal family's first purchase of an electric vehicle, a Jaguar I-Pace, and fought to have the royal train converted to run on used cooking oil, "which actually in the end worked quite well," Charles said. "But I don't know. They say it clogs up the engine or something."

Prince Charles is now grandfather to five, and step-grandfather to how many?

With the arrival of Prince Harry and Meghan Markle's daughter, Prince Charles is a grandfather to William and Kate's kids (George, Charlotte, and Louis) as well as Archie and Lilibet. But he's also step-grandfather to Camilla's grandchildren.

While married to Andrew Parker Bowles, Camilla had two children, Tom and Laura. Tom Parker Bowles, now a cookbook author and food critic, married Sara Buys, senior editor of

British *Town & Country*, in September 2005. The couple separated in 2018, and share two kids together, Lola and Frederick. Art curator and gallery director Laura Parker Bowles (now Laura Lopes) married accountant Harry Lopes in 2006. The couple have three kids, Eliza and twin boys, Gus and Louis.

Prince Charles is also an author, and has written (and co-written) several books about the environment and architecture. He also wrote an illustrated children's book based on stories he used to tell his siblings. What's it called?

*I*n 1980, the Prince of Wales published *The Old Man of Lochnagar*, an illustrated storybook based on childhood fables Charles used to tell Princes Andrew and Edward when they were young. With drawings by Sir Hugh Casson, the book tells the tale of a hermit who lives in a cave in the cliffs surrounding a circular lake, or "corrie loch." The lake sits at the base of Lochnagar, a mountain that overlooks the royal estate at Balmoral in Scotland, where Charles and his family spent their summer holidays.

The Old Man of Lochnagar later inspired a short film, a musical, and even a ballet. The animated short film was produced by the BBC, with Robbie Coltrane as the voice of the old man while

Prince Charles narrated. In the book, the old man wants to escape his neighbors and worries, and he sinks into the lake to go haggis hunting with a Scottish Neptune-like creature that blows bubbles. The TV version changed a few plot points and focused on the later part of the book, where the old man encounters fairylike creatures called "Gorms." He faces trouble when he drains his bathtub and accidentally floods the Gorm kingdom that lives beneath him.

The Prince of Wales isn't the only royal to write a book for kids. Sarah Ferguson and Meghan Markle are also both children's book authors. Charles also co-authored the *Ladybird Expert* series book on climate change and a book about humans' impact on the environment titled *Harmony: A New Way of Looking at Our World*. He also wrote a book about British buildings and urban development titled *A Vision of Britain: A Personal View of Architecture*.

Due to a last-minute change, Prince Charles played a big role in Meghan Markle and Prince Harry's wedding. What was it?

Sadly, the royal bride-to-be had a tumultuous lead-up to the big day. Meghan's father, seventy-three-year-old Thomas Markle, was caught in the middle of a media maelstrom. (See:

staged paparazzi shots of him reading books about England in a coffee shop, an alleged heart attack, and frantic texts sent from Meghan to her dad on the night before her wedding, according to sources.)

On May 17, 2018, just two days before the royal wedding, the bride-to-be released a statement via Twitter: "Sadly, my father will not be able to attend our wedding. I have always cared for my father and hope he can be given the space he needs to focus on his health. I would like to thank everyone who has offered generous messages of support. Please know how much Harry and I look forward to sharing our special day with you on Saturday."

With Meghan's father unable to attend, many speculated whether Meghan would walk herself down the aisle, or be given away by her mother, Doria Ragland, instead. Then on Friday, May 18, Kensington Palace released another statement: "Ms. Meghan Markle has asked His Royal Highness The Prince of Wales to accompany her down the aisle of the Quire of St. George's Chapel on her Wedding Day," the palace said. "The Prince of Wales is pleased to be able to welcome Ms. Markle to The Royal Family in this way."

But while Charles did lend a helping hand—er, elbow—Meghan actually walked herself most of the way. The bride-to-be exited the Rolls-Royce Phantom IV with two page boys—seven-year-old twins Brian and John Mulroney—who helped carry her sixteen-foot veil up the stairs to St. George's, through the entrance, and down the aisle of the nave. Behind her, the eight other page boys and flower girls followed along. Prince Charles joined at the transept, offering his arm and escorting her down through the choir area of the chapel to the altar, where the royal family, as well as Meghan's mother and the couple's friends, were seated. The groom sweetly said "Thank you, Pa," as Charles handed over his bride.

In November 2018, Prince Harry revealed in the BBC documentary *Prince, Son and Heir: Charles at 70* that he was actually the one who asked his father to walk his fiancée down the aisle: "I asked him to and I think he knew it was coming and he immediately said, 'Yes, of course, I'll do whatever Meghan needs and I'm here to support you.' For him, that's a fantastic opportunity to step up and be that support, and you know he's our father so of course he's gonna be there for us." (Of course, according to Harry and Meghan's bombshell interview with Oprah, their relationship with Prince Charles has since soured with Harry admitting that, ahead of his decision to exit the family, he'd had two conversations with Prince Charles "before he stopped taking my calls.")

Prince Charles is the Duke of Cornwall, and therefore in charge of the Duchy of Cornwall, a private estate that generates millions of pounds in income a year. How?

*F*irst, what in the world is a duchy (pronounced "dutch-ee")? Simply stated, a duchy is the territory of a duke or dukedom. While they used to contain only land from the geographic area of the county from which they originated (aka the land of Cornwall or Lancaster), that is no longer the case. The Duchy of Cornwall, for example, owns land in over twenty-three counties. The land varies from farming and residential use to commercial properties and planned developments. The only existing duchies in England today are the Duchy of Lancaster and the Duchy of Cornwall.

The Duchy of Cornwall is always inherited by the eldest son of the reigning monarch, so Prince William will one day become Prince of Wales and Duke of Cornwall, and therefore in charge of the duchy. Thankfully, he's already started prepping: he's sat in on the twice-yearly meetings of the Duchy Council, called the Prince's Council, since 2015.

While the duchy's main job is managing the land investments (currently about 0.2 percent of the UK, with land in Cornwall, Somerset, Devon, Herefordshire, and the Isles of Scilly), the duchy also contains a financial investment portfolio. It has special legal rights and some of the powers of a corporation. One of these is *bona vacantia*, the right to ownerless property. This rule says that the property of anyone who dies in the county of Cornwall without a will or identifiable heirs, as well as assets belonging to dissolved companies whose registered office was in Cornwall, pass to the duchy. Charles has funneled this extra money, sometimes up to thousands of pounds a year, into charitable donations.

Prince Charles uses the duchy's total revenues (about $23.8 million in 2019) to fund his public, charitable, and private activities and those of his family. For example, the duchy helps pay for the offices of the Duke and Duchess of Cambridge, the staff of Prince Charles, the upkeep of the Highgrove House gardens, and more.

PART V

THE QUEEN

Princess Elizabeth was born Elizabeth Alexandra Mary Windsor on April 21, 1926, to her parents, the Duke and Duchess of York. But, at the time, she wasn't in the direct line of succession. How come?

When then Princess Elizabeth was born to Prince Albert, the Duke of York, and his wife, Lady Elizabeth Bowes-Lyon, on April 21, 1926, there wasn't much of a chance she would ever accede to the throne. Prince Albert (his family and friends called him "Bertie") was, of course, the younger son of King George V, which likened Elizabeth to Princesses Beatrice and Eugenie in terms of their position in line. Instead, it was Edward VIII (Prince Albert's older brother) who was the direct heir, with Elizabeth's father up next. Given that Edward was young and healthy and on track to marry and produce an heir, Elizabeth's arrival, while celebrated, was met with significantly less pomp and circumstance.

Instead, Elizabeth came into the world via C-section at 2:40 a.m. She was born at 17 Bruton Street in Mayfair, at the London home of her maternal grandparents, the Earl and Countess of Strathmore, who made their fortune as prominent coal mine owners. Despite her position as third in line, the home secretary, Sir William Joynson-Hicks, still was present to witness the birth, per royal tradition, though many wondered why, given Elizabeth's distant ties to the throne. (That said, she held a prominent place thanks to the 1701 Act of Settlement that made her third in line ahead of her father's younger brothers.)

As crowds gathered and rejoiced, the king and queen arrived to meet the young woman who would be Queen Elizabeth II. Queen Mary described her as a "little darling with a lovely complexion and pretty fair hair" while the Duke of York remarked in a letter to his parents, "We always wanted a child to make our happiness complete." Elizabeth was christened in the private chapel at Buckingham Palace in May as royal baby mania continued to reach a fever pitch. (The crowds on Bruton Street got so rambunctious, Elizabeth's parents had to sneak her out the back entrance to the home just to get some fresh air—proof that no matter the time period, royal babies always carry great amounts of joy.)

Her grandfather, King George V, was the reigning monarch and took delight in his precocious grandchild. What was young Elizabeth's nickname for the king?

When Elizabeth was nearing her first birthday in 1927, royal duty (i.e., a tour of Australia) called her parents away from their much-adored newborn for close to six months.

She was left in the care of her nanny, but also her grandparents on both sides. During that time, the notoriously intense and intimidating King George V developed a bond with Elizabeth. In *Elizabeth & Margaret* by Andrew Morton, he recounted a tale from the Archbishop of Canterbury who said that, on one occasion, the king pretended to be a horse in a game he was playing with Elizabeth. As part of that, she was allowed to pull him around by his gray beard as he shuffled behind on the floor. He had other grandchildren, but somehow, Elizabeth was whom he doted on the most. As Elizabeth grew to be a toddler, she returned his affection, assigning her grandfather a charming (and clever) nickname: Grandpa England.

Of course, Elizabeth also earned a nickname of her own at a young age—and one that has stuck with her for the entirety of her life: Lilibet. Many report that it materialized after a toddler-sized Elizabeth struggled to say her own name. Even after she took the throne, she signed most of her private correspondence using this moniker.

Of course, in Queen Elizabeth II's later years, Lilibet was phased out of use. The only person who reportedly still used the moniker was her beloved husband of seventy-four years, Prince Philip. (He also called her "Cabbage," according to royal biographer Robert Lacey, the English translation of the French expression for "my darling," *mon petit chou*.) In fact, at his funeral in April 2021, Elizabeth added her own tribute atop his coffin at Windsor Castle. According to reports, observers could see a note that she signed "Lilibet," a sweet nod to their intimacy and longevity as she said her final goodbye. That's why it was especially touching that Prince Harry and Meghan Markle opted to name their firstborn daughter after her great-grandmother. (Their daughter's full name is Lilibet Diana Mountbatten-Windsor.)

Princesses Elizabeth and Margaret grew up in "the palace with a number and without a name." Where was it?

When Princess Elizabeth was fourteen months old, she moved into 145 Piccadilly, her parents' first permanent address. It wasn't an official royal residence, but everyone knew who lived in the stone-fronted, five-story house that came to be known as "the palace with a number and without a name." The royal family even referred to their home that way, calling it "One-Four-Five." It had beautiful views of Green Park and could see across to Buckingham Palace, too. Crowds frequently gathered outside—especially after Princess Margaret was born on August 21, 1930—in hopes of catching a glimpse of the princesses at home. Also unique: the lack of security. According to Andrew Morton, it was possible to simply walk up the path and ring one of the two bells by the door (one was marked "Visitors" and the other said "House").

Still, the setting was exactly the environment in which the Duke and Duchess of York wanted to raise their family. From this address, Elizabeth and Margaret were homeschooled and looked after by their Scottish nanny, Marion Crawford. As a family, the Yorks were quite a close-knit bunch, spending evenings dancing and singing together, reading books, and playing games. Elizabeth's dad, still Prince Albert at the time, commonly referred to his family as "we four," a sweet reference to their impenetrable bond. He was set on bringing up his children in a calm and loving environment—the opposite of his childhood with his authoritative and demanding dad—and, together with his wife, aimed to teach his daughters all aspects of royal duty while enlightening them to their immense privilege at the same time.

As for 145 Piccadilly, the home was destroyed by a bomb in October 1940 during the height of World War II. It was rebuilt in 1975 as the InterContinental London Park Lane hotel, a place you can still visit today.

**There was only a four-year age difference between Princess
Elizabeth and her younger sister, Princess Margaret, and
the two shared a close bond. When Elizabeth was just ten,
what event permanently altered their sisterhood?**

*P*rincesses Elizabeth and Margaret spent six blissful years
together before the dynamic of their relationship was
changed forever by their Uncle David—King Edward VIII—
and his decision to abdicate the throne in 1936. Before that
decision was made, Elizabeth and Margaret's upbringing was
relatively low-key, but they were treated very much the same.
They often dressed alike and received a similar education, too.
In fact, despite the four-year age difference, Elizabeth followed
a comparable curriculum to her younger sister, with Margaret
excelling beyond her years.

But then there was news: King Edward VIII (the Duke of
Windsor) announced that he would abdicate, effective
December 10, 1936, to marry the love of his life, Wallis Simpson,
a twice-divorced American. (At the time, with Edward serving
as the nominal head of the Church of England, he was not per-
mitted to marry a divorcée since Simpson's spouse was still
alive.) This meant that only eleven months after David became
king—before his official coronation—Elizabeth and Margaret's

father, Prince Albert, the Duke of York, succeeded his brother and became King George VI.

For Elizabeth and Margaret, this changed everything. The family left 145 Piccadilly and moved into Buckingham Palace, all 775 rooms of it. With that, the heir-and-the-spare dynamic took full effect. Elizabeth was separated from Margaret almost immediately and elevated to her role as heiress presumptive, which impacted not only her schooling, but her daily life. Her dad approached her more seriously, she was made to prioritize the study of history and politics, and she gained other special privileges, many of which were denied to Margaret. For Margaret in particular, her relationship with her sister—now the future queen of England—began to teeter between jealousy and loyalty. As they grew up, their contrasting personalities also began to show: Elizabeth was introverted and put duty above all else; Margaret was an extrovert and an emotional one at that.

From a young age, Princess Elizabeth's fascination with horses and dogs outweighed her interest in academics. What was the name of her first horse?

At age four, the queen was given her first horse, a Shetland pony named Peggy, from her grandfather King George V.

She learned to ride by age six, and is still riding horses into her nineties. She became a skilled equestrian, owner, and breeder of horses of all types—from eventing, showing, and racing to carriage driving and polo. A few of her favorite horses throughout her lifetime are said to be Burmese, a horse she rode for Trooping the Colour for eighteen years; Estimate, which won the Ascot Gold Cup; and Sanction, the last homebred horse she rode before transitioning to riding only ponies in her advancing years ("A little closer to the ground, so to speak," the queen's head groom Terry Pendry told *Horse & Hound*.)

In her former governess's biography, *The Little Princesses*, a young Elizabeth was "very farm-minded." According to "Crawfie," as Elizabeth and Margaret called Marion Crawford, one day Elizabeth firmly declared: "If I am ever Queen, I shall make a law that there must be no riding on Sundays. Horses should have a rest, too. And I shan't let anyone dock their pony's tail." She and Margaret would "feed" and "water" their toy horses every night, taking care to remove their saddles before bed and lining them in rows along the corridor at Buckingham Palace.

The passion carried into her teen years, when Elizabeth would keep a scrapbook of her father's racehorse, Rising Light. "She has had a terrific involvement in racing all her life, and really knows and understands horses," her former Royal Stud manager Sir Michael Oswald told *Horse & Hound*. "And she has a remarkable memory for pedigrees."

But horses aren't the only animals Elizabeth adores. She also famously has a sweet spot for dogs, particularly Pembroke Welsh corgis and dorgis (a mix between a corgi and a dachshund). She's owned thirty corgis since she became queen in 1952, a tradition started by her parents. King George VI brought home a corgi named Dookie when Elizabeth was six years old, and her first corgi that she could call her very own was named Susan, which she was given when she turned eighteen. The queen reportedly stopped breeding corgis in 2015 so they wouldn't outlive her, but she still has one dorgi and one corgi (as of 2021): Candy and Muick.

At the age of fourteen, then Princess Elizabeth gave her first radio broadcast on the BBC's *Children's Hour*. What did she speak about?

When World War II began for Britain on September 3, 1939, Princesses Elizabeth and Margaret left their parents behind at Buckingham Palace and were evacuated to Windsor Castle to avoid the sudden danger of Nazi raids. (Five bombs were dropped on Buckingham Palace almost a year later on September 13, 1940, while King George VI and Queen Elizabeth—Elizabeth and Margaret's mother—were in residence. They were okay and opted to stay put.) Many other children did the same—left London for small towns and safety during the war—and at the suggestion of Prime Minister Winston Churchill, Princess Elizabeth was asked to give her first radio address as part of the BBC's *Children's Hour* as a way to provide comfort and boost morale.

The words she spoke on October 13, 1940, from Windsor Castle included a shout-out to her sister: "Thousands of you in this country have had to leave your homes and be separated from your fathers and mothers. My sister, Margaret Rose, and I feel so much for you, as we know from experience what it means to be away from those you love most of all." For the first of many public addresses that would be given by the eventual queen, the newspaper coverage was positive. There was even a photo of Elizabeth and Margaret side by side at the microphone. King George VI, who was said to be initially reluctant, was in turn quite proud of his eldest daughter's poise.

Queen Elizabeth II recently mentioned the speech she gave over eighty years ago when the COVID-19 pandemic took hold in April 2020. She said, in reference to the UK's sudden and urgent lockdown where so many were again separated from their families and loved ones: "It reminds me of the very first broadcast I made, in 1940, helped by my sister. We, as children, spoke from here at Windsor to children who had been evacuated from their homes and sent away for their own safety. Today, once again, many will feel a painful sense of separation from their loved ones."

Queen Elizabeth II and Prince Philip celebrated seventy-three years of marriage in 2020. At what age—and under what circumstances—did they meet?

The decades-long royal romance first kicked off aboard the royal yacht *Victoria and Albert* in the summer of 1939. The royal family had traveled to Dartmouth in southwest England when they learned from Lord Mountbatten, Prince Philip's uncle and a distant cousin of Queen Elizabeth II, that a couple of cadets on the ship had gotten sick with the mumps and that the princesses should sequester themselves to avoid exposure. That's when an eighteen-year-old Prince Philip got tagged in to entertain both Elizabeth and Margaret. Elizabeth, who was only thirteen at the time, was instantly smitten with the handsome prince, who happened to be sixth in line to the Greek throne. Per her governess, Marion Crawford, Elizabeth couldn't resist his fair hair and blue eyes and, according to the *New York Times*, "flushed whenever his name was mentioned."

After that, the pair continued to correspond with each other, and as World War II began, even with Philip's career in the

British Royal Navy taking off, the two stayed in touch. Letters paved the way for a visit to Windsor Castle, where Philip caught a pantomime performance of *Aladdin*, with Elizabeth starring in the leading role. He continued to carry a photo of her during battle; she had one of him framed on her mantle at Buckingham Palace.

In 1946, Philip proposed at the royal family's estate at Balmoral in Scotland with a three-carat diamond engagement ring featuring stones that were originally part of a tiara that belonged to his mother, Princess Alice of Battenberg. He asked for the king's permission first, which was granted, but only after asking the pair to wait until Elizabeth's twenty-first birthday—which was more than six months away—to make their intention to marry public. (Of course, the media was already salivating to hear news about the status of their courtship—so much so that in September of that same year, Buckingham Palace issued a statement denying their engagement.) While the king gave his blessing and was said to be a fan of Philip, others inside the palace were less than welcoming and expressed concerns about his family's exile from Greece after Philip's uncle King Constantine I abdicated the throne at the end of World War I. Others deemed him "too German," a nod to the fact that three of his brothers-in-law had joined the Nazi party during the war. (To marry Elizabeth, Philip had to renounce his Greek and

Danish titles and become a naturalized British citizen. He even adopted his mother's family's surname, Mountbatten.)

But on July 9, 1947, fresh off a royal tour of South Africa, Elizabeth and Philip's future together was made official. They married at Westminster Abbey on November 20, 1947, a marriage that would last for over seven decades until Prince Philip's passing on April 9, 2021. For Philip, his marriage to Elizabeth placed him in the unique position of prince consort—as the husband of the queen, he was never allowed to be named king consort—but he took it seriously, carving out a role for himself that left him championing a broad range of interests and causes, with an ultimate goal of supporting his wife and the Crown. (Philip was named Duke of Edinburgh on his wedding day, but wasn't officially named Prince of the United Kingdom until 1957.)

Elizabeth described her affection for Philip best at a speech she gave on the occasion of their fiftieth wedding anniversary in 1997: "He is someone who doesn't take easily to compliments, but he has, quite simply, been my strength and stay all these years, and I, and his whole family, and this and many other countries, owe him a debt greater than he would ever claim, or we shall ever know."

Princess Elizabeth's sixteenth birthday marked her first-ever official engagement, but the speech made on her twenty-first birthday is thought to be her most iconic. What did she speak about and why was it significant?

*O*n her sixteenth birthday in 1942, then princess Elizabeth carried out her first official royal engagement—an inspection of the Grenadier Guards. But it was the speech she made on her twenty-first birthday in South Africa that would cement her legacy as monarch.

In fact, it was the king's idea to embark on the fourteen-week trip as a family following the end of World War II. He wanted to thank the South African people for their support during the war, but he also used it as a way to encourage Elizabeth to mull over her marriage proposal from Prince Philip, which came just months before. But there was even more to the story than that: the trip was an opportunity to showcase King George VI, whose health was already showing signs of declining, side by side with his daughter, who one day would ascend the throne.

That's where Elizabeth's speech came in. She was prepped that on her birthday she'd be delivering the address and was made to spend hours rehearsing until she was deemed ready and confident enough to share her remarks. Broadcast by radio from the government house in Cape Town to an audience of two hundred million people, and with her sister Princess Margaret by her side, it was the moment Elizabeth was first heard dedicating her life to the Crown. She said: "I declare before you all that my whole life, whether it be long or short, shall be devoted to your service and the service of our great imperial family to which we all belong. But I shall not have the strength to carry out this resolution alone unless you join in it with me, as I now invite you to do." She also made it clear that she would strive for racial inclusion and welcomed the "opportunity to speak to all peoples of the British Commonwealth and Empire, wherever they may live, whatever race they come from and whatever language they speak." (Of course, apartheid was made law not long after the royal tour concluded.)

Now, as Elizabeth nears her Platinum Jubilee in 2022, it is this speech that gets referenced the most as the reason she will never abdicate.

At her wedding to Prince Philip, the bride was a vision in Norman Hartnell. But what happened to Queen Mary's Fringe tiara—Princess Elizabeth's headpiece of choice—en route to the ceremony?

When Elizabeth married the love of her life, Lieutenant Philip Mountbatten, on November 20, 1947, it was at the end of the devastation of World War II and at the beginning of Britain's long and hard postwar era. The occasion of their nuptials was said to lift the spirit of the nation, as Winston Churchill dubbed their love for each other "a flash of color on the hard road we have to travel." Much attention was placed on Elizabeth's choice of a wedding dress—an ivory silk Norman Hartnell design that was inspired by Botticelli's famous Renaissance painting Primavera, which symbolized the coming of spring, complete with a thirteen-foot train—so much that, after his design was selected, the windows of his studio had to be whitewashed to ensure secrecy. Not only that, but given the hardships of the war, even the future queen had to use rationing coupons to cover the cost, although the government granted her two hundred extra for her wedding dress. (Hundreds of women, eagerly anticipating the royal wedding, sent their own coupons to Elizabeth, which she had to return.)

Even in times of austerity, the wedding, which was attended by 2,500 guests, went off without a hitch...except for one minor detail. On the way to the ceremony at Westminster Abbey, the headpiece Elizabeth had selected—Queen Mary's fringe tiara, which had been crafted by Garrard & Co. in 1919 from a diamond necklace given to Mary on her wedding day in 1893 by Queen Victoria—snapped. The Crown Jeweller had to be summoned to repair it under pressure. As the House of Garrard website describes it, Elizabeth was "determined to wear this tiara on her special day" so "the princess's tiara was rushed away by a police escort to the Garrard workshop, where it was repaired in haste and returned just in time for the ceremony." In photos, if you look closely, you can even notice a slight difference in the spacing between the diamond spears.

It also wasn't the last time we've seen the tiara. Elizabeth's daughter, Princess Anne, wore it for her wedding to Mark Phillips in 1973, and, more recently, Elizabeth's granddaughter, Princess Beatrice, donned the sparkling headpiece for her own micro wedding in 2020 to Edoardo Mapelli Mozzi.

In 1948, Princess Elizabeth gave birth to her first child, Prince Charles, and in 1950, Princess Anne arrived. But her hands-off role as a parent is one of the more controversial conversations about her. How come?

*I*t was less than two years after the birth of Princess Anne that Elizabeth became queen. From that moment on, her duties were her number one priority, and she often left Charles and Anne in the care of their nannies as well as with her own mother. (This is often cited as the reason Charles and the Queen Mother developed such a close bond.) Immediately after her coronation as queen, Elizabeth's role as monarch overshadowed her role as mum. She kicked off a six-month tour of the Commonwealth, leaving Charles and Anne in the care of royal staffers. For Elizabeth, this was simply how it was done. Her parents hadn't dragged her and her sister Margaret along on international royal tours. But as Charles lamented to his biographer Jonathan Dimbleby in 1994, some of the biggest milestones of childhood were witnessed not by his parents, but by his nannies.

While the queen was away, Prince Philip was put in charge of most major decisions relating to the kids. While Elizabeth enjoyed the time she had to spend with her children over breakfast and following afternoon tea, she had very little of it.

She was also less than affectionate publicly, the polar opposite of her daughter-in-law Diana. (Take the moment the queen reunited with Charles for the first time after her tour of the Commonwealth: she shook his hand.)

The queen—who was also said to exhibit a lack of confidence when it came to parenting her firstborn kids, Charles and Anne—was much more hands-on when it came to raising her sons Prince Andrew, who arrived a decade after Anne in 1960, and Prince Edward, who was born in 1964. Charles in particular has been vocal over the years about the distance he felt from both his mother and Philip.

On the flip side, Anne has often defended her mother's maternal instinct: "We as children may have not been too demanding in the sense that we understand what the limitations were in time and the responsibilities placed on her as monarch in the things she had to do and the travels she had to make. But I don't believe any of us for a second thought she didn't care for us in exactly the same way as any other mother did," the Princess Royal told the BBC. Lord Mountbatten also once reported, according to historian Robert Lacey, that the queen's favorite night of the week was the one when the children's nanny was off. On those nights "Elizabeth could kneel beside the bath, bathe her babies, read to them and put them to bed herself," he explained.

Princess Elizabeth has only ever lived outside the UK once, and it's been said that her time in that country was one of the happiest of her life. Where was it?

*O*ne-way ticket to Malta, please. Then Princess Elizabeth and Prince Philip lived in the small island country off the southern coast of Sicily and North Africa from 1949 to 1951, and it was reportedly some of the happiest times for the young couple. The couple lived in a palazzo-style home just outside Malta's capital of Valletta.

Philip was a lieutenant in the Royal Navy on HMS *Chequers* (later the HMS *Magpie*), which was, at that time, stationed in the Mediterranean. While there, the couple stayed in the eighteen-room Villa Guardamangia belonging to Philip's uncle Lord Mountbatten, who leased the villa starting in the 1920s after being stationed on the small Mediterranean island himself. The 16,000-square-foot villa was referred to by the queen as a "town house," though it was more substantial than that. It had large living quarters, stables for animals, a walled garden with a terrace walkway (the perfect backdrop for the couple's photos while there), and a war shelter.

With relatively little press and attention, Elizabeth and Philip were able to live like "ordinary" people. "The queen really loved living in Malta because she was able to lead a normal life, wander through the towns, and go shopping," Lady Pamela Hicks, one of the queen's bridesmaids, said in an interview. "It was the only place that she was able to live the life of a naval officer's wife, just like all the other wives." The future queen hosted tea parties for service wives, and local papers documented people turning up at the villa to gift her fresh oranges. She also was said to enjoy the local cinema, picnics in the countryside, and swimming at Sliema beach, three miles from her home.

The couple have been back since: They celebrated their second wedding anniversary on the island, as well as their sixtieth wedding anniversary in 2007. Queen Elizabeth visited her former home of Villa Guardamangia during her state visit to Malta in 1992. The queen said she and Philip had a "deep affection for your country and the outgoing, generous Maltese people who have always offered us the hand of friendship," during a state banquet in 2005. During a 2015 visit, she remarked, "Visiting Malta is always very special for me. I remember happy days here with Prince Philip when we were first married."

Villa Guardamangia was put up for sale in 2019, though much of the building's contents, including furniture, artwork, and antiques, were sold at auction. Following a campaign for the building to be restored and opened to the public, it was acquired by the government of Malta in October 2019, with restorations underway. Reportedly, the queen will be invited back once the renovations are complete.

It's a moment she herself described as one of the "most exciting nights" of her life, when Princesses Elizabeth and Margaret were allowed to leave the palace incognito. On what occasion did this take place?

On May 8, 1945, aka VE Day, a nineteen-year-old Elizabeth and fourteen-year-old Margaret, disguised as members of the public, left Buckingham Palace to mingle with the jubilant crowds celebrating the end of World War II and victory over Germany. On the balcony of Buckingham Palace earlier that day, Elizabeth and Margaret stood with their parents and Sir Winston Churchill to watch the throngs of joyous crowds, emerging onto the balcony every hour to wave amid cheers from the people down below. Elizabeth wore her Auxiliary Territorial Service (ATS) uniform, as she was the first female of the British royal family to serve in the armed forces.

Later that night, the teenage girls left the palace (with a slew of guards, ladies-in-waiting, and the king's equerry, Peter Townsend) and danced the conga up Piccadilly and St. James's Street, crammed in among the public, their party numbering sixteen in total. "I remember we were terrified of being recognized, so I pulled my uniform cap well down over my eyes," the queen stated during a BBC radio broadcast recorded in 1985 for the fortieth anniversary of VE Day.

The crowds chanted, "We want the king!" and Elizabeth's parents reemerged on the balcony. "We cheered the king and queen on the balcony and then walked miles through the streets," the queen recalled during the broadcast. "I remember lines of unknown people linking arms and walking down Whitehall, all of us just swept along on a tide of happiness and relief."

"It was a view of their parents that the princesses had never before experienced," Margaret Elphinstone (later Rhodes), a cousin to Elizabeth and Margaret, wrote in her 2011 memoir *The Final Curtsey: A Royal Memoir by the Queen's Cousin.* She also wrote that the "unique burst of freedom" for her cousins was like "a Cinderella moment in reverse, in which they could pretend they were ordinary and unknown." Elizabeth enjoyed the revelry so much she later described it as "one of the most memorable nights of my life," for a 1985 BBC recording. The sisters repeated their breakout the following evening, and the night of and night after VJ Day on August 15 and 16, 1945.

During WWII, then Princess Elizabeth had served in a reserve unit in the war and was also named colonel of the Grenadier

Guards. She first joined the ATS in 1945 at age eighteen, where she learned to drive and maintain vehicles for the British Army. A 1947 issue of *Collier's* magazine wrote of the princess: "One of her major joys was to get dirt under her nails and grease stains in her hands, and display these signs of labor to her friends."

When Princess Elizabeth got the devastating news that her father, King George VI, had passed away in his sleep, she was out of town. Where was she and what was she doing at the time?

Elizabeth and her family knew for quite some time that her father's health was declining. In 1949, he suffered an arterial blockage and had his left lung removed in 1951. But that didn't mean she was emotionally prepared when news came that her father had passed while she was on a tour of Kenya with Philip in February 1952.

The king himself had seen them off as they embarked on their trip, flying from London Airport to Nairobi on January 31. He was battling lung cancer at the time, but he made the effort to be there and wave goodbye to his daughter for the last time. The trip was an important one, but also came at a dangerous time in the British colony. Mau Mau fighters were gaining power in their fight for independence (they won in 1963), and there was a lot of concern for the princess's safety during the tour, but they still went forward with the trip, since it was deemed a politically bad move to cancel it.

Upon arrival, Elizabeth—just twenty-five at the time—and Philip visited Nairobi National Park, then stayed at the Sagana hunting lodge, which had been gifted to them as a wedding present by Kenya. John Jochimsen, one of the press photographers shadowing the pair on the tour, described their energy at the start of the tour: "I remember the Princess at the time being very happy and carefree—she hadn't been married long and didn't have the weight on her shoulders as she would on becoming Queen." But while the queen was enjoying the diversions of their visit (like a close encounter with rampaging elephants ahead of their stay at Treetops Hotel in Aberdare National Park on February 5), the king died peacefully in his sleep during the early hours of February 6.

It was Philip who broke the news to his wife after learning about it from a local journalist. According to reports, the news was released to the press, by accident, before the queen was informed. A telegram had been sent, but it couldn't be decoded because the keys to the safe holding the codebook were unavailable. When Philip was finally informed, his private secretary, Commander Michael Parker said, "He looked as if you'd dropped half the world on him. He took [Elizabeth] up to the garden and they walked up and down the lawn while he talked and talked and talked to her." Plans for "Hyde Park Corner"—the code name for arrangements following the death of the king—were already underway.

After taking in the news, Elizabeth wrote letters apologizing that she had to cancel the rest of the tour before leaving the hotel to return to England. She also had a single request—that no photographs be snapped of her exit. As a result, there isn't a single shot of her in those first few hours as monarch. As Sir Harold Nicolson, a diplomat and politician, described it, "Princess Elizabeth is flying back from Kenya. She became queen while perched in a tree in Africa, watching the rhinoceros come down to the pool to drink." Then, there were the words of Winston Churchill during a broadcast to the nation: "During these last days, the king walked with death, as if death were a companion, an acquaintance whom he recognized and did not fear... I, whose youth was passed in the august, unchallenged, and tranquil glories of the Victorian era, may well feel a thrill of invoking, once more, the prayer and the anthem: God Save the Queen."

Even though she was named queen the minute her father passed away, sixteen months went by before Queen Elizabeth II's coronation. How come?

*T*he queen's official coronation was held on June 2, 1953—more than a year after her father passed away on February 6, 1952. Although she became Queen Elizabeth II the minute King George VI died, that's only because the throne is never left vacant. But it's thought to be disrespectful to not allow an adequate period of mourning to take place before crowning the next sovereign. (For King Edward VII, nearly nineteen months went by between his ascension and coronation; for King George VI—Elizabeth's dad—it was just under sixteen months before his coronation took place.)

More than eight thousand people turned out to watch Elizabeth's coronation ceremony in person, despite the fact that it poured the entire day. While many spent the night camped out along the Mall by Buckingham Palace, eager to catch a glimpse of the queen as she passed by with Philip in a gilded coach, twenty-seven million people in the UK watched the three-hour ceremony from home. After all, this coronation was the first ever to be televised. (TV sales skyrocketed as a result.)

En route to the ceremony, Elizabeth wore the George IV State Diadem crown atop her head, which features 1,333 diamonds and 169 pearls. But when the ceremony kicked off at Westminster Abbey, it was St. Edward's Crown that was placed on her head during the coronation service. The queen also fittingly wore a dress by her go-to designer Norman Hartnell. It was made from white satin and embroidered with the emblems of the United Kingdom and the Commonwealth in gold and silver thread. Led by the Archbishop of Canterbury, the ceremony was organized into six different parts: the recognition, the oath, the anointing, the investiture (the part that includes the crowning), the enthronement, and the homage. More than 250 people participated in the proceedings.

Still, much of the coverage of the proceedings noted the familial touches—the moment when the Duke of Edinburgh kneeled down before his wife as he pledged his whole life to her service and defense; the inclusion of Prince Charles, who was just four years old, who oscillated between boredom, irritation, and excitement, especially by the time he (along with his sister, Princess Anne) was brought out on the balcony with his parents to watch the Royal Air Force jet planes fly across the Mall. Overall, the occasion was a huge success, the beginning of a new era for the monarchy and one that would place Elizabeth on the throne for nearly seventy years and counting.

Early on in her reign, Queen Elizabeth II was put in the position of having to give her sister Princess Margaret permission to marry the love of her life, Peter Townsend, despite the fact that he was divorced. What compromise did the queen offer and Margaret subsequently reject?

*I*t was the stuff royal fairy tales were made of: A twenty-two-year-old Princess Margaret fell in love with Peter Townsend, a man who served as equerry to her father, King George VI, and eventually to Queen Elizabeth II, and who first met Margaret when she was just fourteen. (He later said of Margaret that she was "as one would expect of a fourteen-year-old girl.") Still, when King George passed away, a romance blossomed, and on the queen's coronation day, the world became aware of their love affair thanks to a simple and ever-so-subtle gesture: The princess flicked a piece of fluff from his uniform while waiting outside Westminster Abbey. It wasn't long before news of their romance became front-page news.

But there was a problem: Peter was divorced. He had married Cecil Rosemary Pawle in 1941 after serving in the Indian Civil Service, and the couple had two sons together, but when Cecil had an affair, Peter filed for divorce. (It was made official in November 1952, just ahead of his confirmed romance with Margaret—although the pair are rumored to have begun dating as early as 1947.) That's when trouble arose. Since Margaret was only twenty-two, she needed the queen's consent in order to marry under the Royal Marriages Act of 1772. And since Elizabeth was also head of the Church of England, which was adamantly against divorce, she refused to grant Margaret permission to marry Peter—but it wasn't an outright "no." At the time, Elizabeth encouraged Margaret and Peter to delay their marriage until Margaret was twenty-five and had the option to choose her groom for herself.

When the clock struck twenty-five for Margaret, they still were denied permission to wed. Instead, a compromise was suggested by both Elizabeth and Prime Minister Anthony Eden (who also happened to be divorced and remarried himself): Margaret could marry Peter...but she had to remove herself and her children from the line of succession, therefore making the queen's permission unnecessary. As Eden described it in a letter to Commonwealth prime ministers, the Royal Marriages Act was the problem. "Her Majesty would not wish to stand in the way of her sister's happiness," he said.

With plans being drawn up to move forward, suddenly Margaret changed her decision. She released a statement: "I would like it to be known that I have decided not to marry Group Captain Peter Townsend. I have been aware that, subject to my renouncing my rights of succession, it might have been possible for me to contract a civil marriage. But, mindful of the Church's teaching that Christian marriage is indissoluble, and conscious of my duty to the Commonwealth, I have decided to put these considerations before any others." A letter uncovered in 2009 suggests that Margaret was placing quite a bit of weight on an intended meeting with Peter in October 1955, writing: "But it is only by seeing him in this way that I feel I can properly decide whether I can marry him or not." By the end of the month, their intentions to wed were called off, and Margaret instead went on to marry Antony Armstrong-Jones (Lord Snowdon) in 1960. (The pair had two kids together and later divorced.)

Still, Peter is often considered to be the love of Margaret's life. But as Peter later wrote in a memoir he published, called *Time and Chance*, "I simply hadn't the weight, I knew it, to counter-balance all she would have lost."

The queen's birthday is in April, but it's celebrated in June. Why is that?

*Y*ou can still sing "Happy Birthday, Ma'am!" on April 21. There are also private celebrations and gun salutes in Hyde Park, Windsor Great Park, and the Tower of London in April. But the queen's official birthday is actually celebrated in June, mostly because April's weather can be hit-or-miss (no, seriously). The monarchs' birthdays have been celebrated as separate days from their actual birthdays since 1748, during the reign of King George II. The tradition started in order to align the celebrations with a higher probability of good weather (at least in the Northern Hemisphere) for outdoor ceremonies.

Since then, the date of the monarch's birthday has been determined throughout the British Empire, and later the Commonwealth, either by royal proclamation issued by the sovereign, or by statute laws passed by Parliament. In the UK and a few other countries, the queen's official birthday is a public holiday.

Edward VII, the great-grandfather of Queen Elizabeth II, reigned from 1901 to 1910. His birthday was in November, so he moved his birthday ceremony to summer in the hopes of better weather. Elizabeth's father followed suit, since his actual birthday was in December. Originally, the queen's official birthday was celebrated on the second Thursday of June—the same day that her father, King George VI, celebrated his official birthday during his reign.

However, this was changed in 1959, seven years after she became queen. Now, Elizabeth's official birthday is celebrated on the second Saturday of June with Trooping the Colour, aka the Queen's Birthday Parade, in London. The Queen's Birthday Honours, a list of awards and appointments, is also announced during the month of the queen's official birthday celebrations.

Of her many royal homes, Queen Elizabeth II always spends Christmas where?

Spending the winter holidays at Sandringham is a tradition for Queen Elizabeth II. The property was acquired by the royal family in 1862 as a country home for King Edward VII, and was then passed down to each subsequent monarch. Elizabeth's grandfather and father both spent their final moments at Sandringham, and it's where Elizabeth gave her first Christmas broadcast in 1957. The queen likes to spend until February at the Norfolk estate, where she honors the anniversary of her father's passing in private with her family.

Sandringham is about one hundred miles from London and the site of the royal fruit farms, which have been mostly converted to organic farming practices. It also boasts an apple juice pressery, a sawmill, museum, restaurant, and wild shooting grounds (for which it is most well-known). Additionally, it's the site of the royals' annual walk to Christmas Day services at St. Mary Magdalene Church on the grounds of Sandringham Estate. It's also the estate on which Anmer Hall, the Cambridges' country home, sits.

Then there's Balmoral Castle, the Queen's Scottish highland home, where she's known to spend the latter part of summer.

It's believed to be her favorite of the royal residences, namely because it's a place where the royals (and their pets) often unwind and are in relative seclusion, and it's far less opulent than Buckingham or Windsor. At Balmoral, the schedule for the day is driving the Land Rover, fishing, hunting, walking through the picturesque highlands, parlor games, and outdoor lunches and barbecues. In the documentary *Our Queen at 90*, Princess Eugenie said of Balmoral, "I think Granny is the most happy there."

Unlike Windsor Castle and Buckingham Palace, Sandringham and Balmoral are private residences of the queen. There's also the Palace of Holyroodhouse in Edinburgh, Scotland, and Hillsborough Castle in Northern Ireland. Both are her residences when she makes official visits to those countries. Hillsborough Castle, built in the 1770s, is also the official residence of Northern Ireland's secretary of state. The grounds include one hundred acres of lush gardens.

And, of course, there's Buckingham Palace. It's the 775-room London residence and administrative headquarters of the monarchy, located in the City of Westminster at the end of the Mall that runs from the Admiralty Arch to the Victoria Memorial. The queen carries out her ceremonial and official duties from Buckingham, and it's where she meets the prime minister for weekly audiences and hosts investitures in the ballroom. During World War II, the palace was bombed nine times.

The queen left Buckingham during the beginning of the COVID-19 pandemic to quarantine at Windsor Castle, about an hour's drive from Buckingham, where she stayed for the remainder of 2020 and into most of 2021. Windsor Castle has one thousand rooms and is the largest occupied castle in the world. The queen first lived at Windsor with her sister, Margaret, during WWII. She visits frequently on the weekends after conducting official business from Buckingham Palace during the week.

The queen "broke royal protocol" at the funeral of Sir Winston Churchill, someone she greatly admired. What did she do?

While Her Majesty is usually the last person to arrive at any ceremony or function, the queen broke protocol by arriving before Sir Winston Churchill's family and his coffin at his funeral on January 30, 1965, as a sign of respect for the late prime minister. She also arranged for Churchill to have a state funeral, a rarity for someone who is not a member of the royal family. As of 2021, his was the last state funeral in the UK (Princess Diana, the Queen Mother, and Prince Philip all had "ceremonial funerals").

According to the documentary *Elizabeth: Our Queen*, Churchill's grandson, Sir Nicholas Soames, said, "It is absolutely exceptional if not unique for the queen to grant precedence to anyone. For her to arrive before the coffin and before my grandfather was a beautiful and very touching gesture."

As Elizabeth's first prime minister after her ascension in February 1952, Sir Winston Churchill held a special place in the queen's heart and had a profound effect on her life and legacy. He was a counselor to her father, led the country to victory in WWII, offered guidance on the inner workings of politics and duty to the newly anointed queen, and even pressed Elizabeth to keep the family name of Windsor when her father died. ("House of Mountbatten" was encouraged by her uncle, Lord Mountbatten.)

In his final toast to her as prime minister, Churchill said: "Never have the august duties which fall upon the British monarchy been discharged with more devotion than in the brilliant opening to Your Majesty's reign. We thank God for the gift he has bestowed upon us and vow ourselves anew to the sacred cause, and wise and kindly way of life of which Your Majesty is the young, gleaming champion."

According to issue 135 of *Finest Hour, The Journal of Winston Churchill*, Elizabeth sent a handwritten letter in response, assuring him that no subsequent prime minister would "be able to hold the place of my first prime minister to whom both my husband and I owe so much and for whose wise guidance during the early years of my reign I shall always be so profoundly grateful."

What 1966 event is said to be Queen Elizabeth II's biggest regret of her entire reign?

*F*or fans of *The Crown*, the Aberfan disaster was one of the most memorable and gut-wrenching episodes of the show. On October 21, 1966, at approximately 9:00 a.m., a colliery spoil tip (a pile of waste material that gets removed during mining) located directly above Aberfan, a mining village in South Wales, suddenly slid downhill. A total of 144 people were killed—116 of which were children.

The worst part was that concerns had been expressed about the spoil tip's location above not only the village, but the local junior school that was hit hardest when the disaster occurred. The collapse was said to have been caused by a buildup of rainfall after an especially stormy period in the region. The timing of it was also thought to be the most tragic part. If the spoil tip had come loose just thirty minutes earlier, none of the children would have been in the classroom, which would have meant many lives spared.

As for the queen's role, she didn't visit Aberfan until eight days after the tragedy occurred on October 29. Biographer Sally Bedell Smith said in *Elizabeth the Queen: The Life of a Modern Monarch* that the reason for the delay was that she didn't want the focus to be on her when it should have been on locating children still missing in the rubble. On the contrary, Prince Philip went almost immediately on October 22 as did Lord Snowdon, Princess Margaret's husband, who visited the families of the missing as soon as he heard the news. And while many pressured Elizabeth to make the trip straight away, she continually declined, according to royal advisors. When she finally did make the trip, the people of Aberfan said the sight of her was a great comfort. Others remembered seeing the usually stoic queen cry.

To this day, her decision to delay her visit is often reported as one of her greatest regrets. Throughout her reign, she has gone back to Aberfan several times, including a trip she made with Charles to mark the fiftieth anniversary of the disaster in 2016.

In 1968, Queen Elizabeth II permitted cameras to film her family for the BBC documentary *Royal Family*. Why was it locked away, no longer available for viewing, soon after it aired?

*I*t was intended as an effort to humanize the queen: a fly-on-the-wall documentary of the royal family at home that would show them as real people, not untouchable (and out-of-touch) royalty. After all, it was the 1960s and the era of free love. An institution as archaic as the monarchy needed to find a way to prove their relevance. TV as a medium seemed the perfect fit.

The queen was initially reluctant, but at the urging of her press secretary William Heseltine, she agreed to participate. Philip was already on board and took on the role of orchestrating all the details. The idea was to use the documentary not only as a way to pull the curtain back on life at Buckingham Palace—and Balmoral, too—but also to introduce the world to Prince Charles, just twenty-one years old at the time, who was nearing his investiture as Prince of Wales. Despite pushback from other family members (Princess Anne openly discussed her reservations later on saying, "I never liked the idea of *Royal Family*. I thought it was a rotten idea."), filming moved forward with the chief of the BBC's documentary unit, Richard Cawston, at the helm of the project.

A total of forty-three hours of footage was shot over the course of a year beginning on June 8, 1968, at the Trooping the Colour ceremony. Locations ranged from Windsor Castle to the royal train and the yacht. Some of the more iconic moments included the queen taking Prince Edward to a candy store to buy ice cream (with actual cash), Prince Philip manning the barbeque at Balmoral, and Prince Charles water-skiing. There's even footage of Elizabeth making small talk with US President Richard Nixon: "World problems are so complex, aren't they now?" (Again, this was the first time the royal family was seen *and* heard—a big deal at the time.)

More than thirty million viewers tuned in for the film's debut on June 21, 1969. At the time of its airing, it was considered a major success, but positive reviews soon devolved into criticism and many felt that the power and effect of the royal family had been compromised. In 1972, the film (and any unused footage) was locked away in the royal archives and was never to be aired again without the queen's explicit permission. Snippets from the film have been aired on occasion such as the queen's Diamond Jubilee and a 2011 documentary called *The Duke at 90*. But other than a recent breach that had the film available to view online in its entirety—but only temporarily— it has remained in the vault.

Fact-checking *The Crown*: Did Queen Elizabeth really subject Margaret Thatcher to "the Balmoral test"?

Margaret Thatcher, Britain's first female prime minister, did visit the royal family at Balmoral Castle during her tenure, just like other previous prime ministers. (Another fun fact: the queen has counseled fourteen prime ministers during her reign.)

In season four of *The Crown*, the PM and her husband Denis undergo "the Balmoral test" (as does Lady Diana), a series of activities and social outings full of unspoken, unofficial protocol like dress code and conversation. So was there really such a thing as "the Balmoral test," and did Thatcher really fail so miserably?

Thatcher never mentioned her trips to Balmoral in her memoirs, and she rarely mentioned the queen. In *The Iron Lady*, biographer John Campbell wrote: "Mrs Thatcher loathed having to go once a year to Balmoral. She had no interest in horses, dogs or country sports and regarded the outdoor life—long walks and picnics in all weathers—which the Royal Family enjoyed on holiday, as 'purgatory.'"

According to Ben Pimlott's biography *The Queen*, a former Whitehall official said the Thatchers' attendance at Philip's outdoor barbecues was full of awkward moments: "Monarch and consort cooking sausages for the disconcerted premier and her husband on a windswept hillside, each couple trying desperately to be informal." Thatcher reportedly neglected to pack appropriate walking shoes, instead borrowing Wellies (rain boots). When the last day of her trip arrived, Thatcher would arrange to leave at 6:00 a.m. "She couldn't get away fast enough," said the official.

Biographer Andrew Morton wrote in his book *Diana: Her True Story*: "The very quirks and obscure family traditions which have accrued over the years can intimidate newcomers. 'Don't sit there' they chorus at an unfortunate guest foolish enough to try and sit in a chair in the drawing room which was last used by Queen Victoria. Those who successfully navigate this social minefield, popularly known as 'the Balmoral test,' are accepted by the royal family. The ones who fail vanish from royal favour as quickly as the Highland mists come and go."

One of the biggest security breaches of the queen's reign occurred in 1982. What happened?

*A*t around 7:00 a.m. on July 9, 1982, a thirty-three-year-old man named Michael Fagan scaled Buckingham Palace's fourteen-foot outer wall and climbed up a drainpipe in what became known as the worst royal security breach of all time. After wandering about the palace corridors for awhile, breaking an ashtray in one of the rooms and cutting his hand on the broken glass, and checking out King George V's multi-million-dollar stamp collection, he made his way to the queen's bedroom and pulled the curtains open on her four-poster bed. For what it's worth, the queen was ever-so-stylish; Fagan said in a 2012 interview with the *Independent* that Her Majesty was wearing a knee-length nightie in a Liberty of London print.

Accounts of his discovery in the queen's bedroom differ: Some say Queen Elizabeth II only called security when Fagan got up, and that he was found sitting on the edge of her bed. Fagan himself insists the queen immediately left the room to find a guard soon after he entered. She had phoned the palace switchboard twice for police, but none arrived. A chambermaid arrived ten minutes later, followed by one of her footmen, who'd been walking her dogs. Two minutes passed before two policemen arrived and apprehended Fagan.

The security breach was unheard of: While an alarm sensor had gone off, palace guards believed it was faulty and silenced it multiple times. And this wasn't the first time Fagan had broken in. The month prior, he had scaled a drainpipe and climbed in through an unlocked window on the roof. When a housemaid saw him and called security, he disappeared, and guards doubted the maid's story. But Fagan had accomplished quite a bit on his first royal break-in: he drank half a bottle of wine from Prince Charles's royal apartments, ate cheese and crackers, sat on the throne, and searched endlessly for a bathroom.

Fagan was later committed to a psychiatric hospital—but not arrested, he was only charged with theft of the half-drank wine bottle, but those charges were later dropped—before being released in January 1983. In a 2012 interview, Fagan said he was on "bad mushrooms" when he broke in and met the queen. The scandal led the queen's top security brass to offer resignations, and guards' presence surrounding and within the palace was beefed up considerably.

Queen Elizabeth II was criticized for the way she handled the death of her daughter-in-law Princess Diana. How come?

*W*hen the queen's former daughter-in-law Princess Diana was killed at the age of thirty-six in a car crash in the Pont de l'Alma tunnel in Paris, France, on August 31, 1997, the world erupted with an outpouring of shock and grief. But there was also a great deal of confusion in regard to the queen's reaction. The famously unemotional Elizabeth appeared to be going about her business as usual, as far as the public's perception of it went. Hours after Princes William and Harry—who were with Prince Charles and the queen at Balmoral—learned the news, she took them to church. Elizabeth also opted to stay in Scotland for days rather than return to London, the center of a nation in mourning. "Show us you care," the tabloid headlines famously read.

Eventually, she did—returning to London five days after Diana's passing to walk among the crowds leaving flowers at the gates of Buckingham Palace and chat with them about the impact of the loss. During those conversations, many reported how sad she was and also that there were tears welling in her eyes. On September 6, 1997, she made a special televised address—

broadcast live from the balcony at Buckingham Palace—in an effort to connect with her public. In it, she attempted to explain her absence: "We have all been trying in our different ways to cope. It is not easy to express a sense of loss, since the initial shock is often succeeded by a mixture of other feelings: disbelief, incomprehension, anger—and concern for those who remain. We have all felt those emotions in these last few days."

She went on to praise Diana and share her concern for William and Harry. "Diana was an exceptional and gifted human being. In good times and bad, she never lost her capacity to smile and laugh, nor to inspire others with her warmth and kindness. I admired and respected her for her energy and commitment to others, especially for her devotion to her two boys." It was only the second time in the queen's reign that she had made a special address to the nation, aside from her annual Christmas broadcasts. (The first time she gave a special address was in 1991 when she asked the nation to keep soldiers participating in the Gulf War in their prayers.)

A palace spokesperson also acknowledged that the queen was hurt at the suggestion that she was indifferent to those in mourning. (A fictionalized account of the queen's reaction to Diana's death is available in the 2006 movie *The Queen*.)

Queen Elizabeth II famously wears vibrant pastels and neon colors for almost all royal occasions so that she can be seen, no matter your position in the crowd. But that's not the only quirk about her wardrobe. What's the deal with her purse?

*I*t may be the queen's most famous line: "I have to be seen to be believed." Hence, a public wardrobe composed almost entirely of bright neon colors that can be spotted on a 5'4" woman in a carriage or on a balcony from a mile away. That way, jostled onlookers can go home and tell their friends and family: "I saw the queen!" It also brings excitement to the mundane: yet another ribbon cutting or plaque unveiling feels that much more attention-worthy when the monarch is wearing a jolt of bright canary yellow.

Besides her iconic pastels, bright florals, and eye-popping neon coat dresses, Queen Elizabeth II has a few other style signatures, including her matching hats (most often by Philip Treacy), gloves by Cornelia James, low-heeled pumps by Anello & Davide, nude hosiery, and Launer handbags. But her purse isn't only used as an accessory. The queen reportedly signals courtiers with her bag, though always extremely discreetly. When she switches the purse from left to right arm, she's supposedly ready to end the current conversation. If her purse is placed on the table during a meal, she'd like the event to wrap up in five minutes; if placed on the floor, she's ready to be tactfully rescued by her lady-in-waiting ASAP.

Other former dressers to the queen include Norman Hartnell (who designed her wedding and coronation dresses), Hardy Amies, and Angela Kelly, author of the biography *The Other Side of the Coin: The Queen, the Dresser and the Wardrobe*, who was personally granted permission to pen the tome by the queen herself. The royal dressers know better than anyone that her clothes serve a specific purpose: she must be able to wave endlessly (hence, coats and dresses cut with generous armholes), stand for hours (shoes that are broken in by ladies-in-waiting before she wears them), and avoid embarrassing wardrobe malfunctions (cue the use of weighted skirt hems).

When in private, she opts for tweed, tartan, jodhpurs, silk headscarves, and waxed-cotton Barbour jackets or trench coats. But believing that she cares little about fashion is a mistake, said Andrew Bolton, curator of the costume institute at the Metropolitan Museum of Art. "She is not particularly interested in high fashion, but she is particular about clothes and interested in things that make her absolutely identifiable as queen," he told the *New York Times* in 2012.

Her Diamond Jubilee year also coincided with this major world event. What was it?

$\mathcal{T}$he queen's Diamond Jubilee, marking sixty years on the throne, coincided with the 2012 Summer Olympics in London. The result? A giant celebration to honor the British people and their long-reigning sovereign. Events were held throughout the year, and royal family members toured the UK and Commonwealth countries as representatives of Her Majesty. It also marked the beginning of withdrawal from public life for the Duke of Edinburgh, who officially wrapped up his public duties in 2017.

And who could forget that grand entrance during the Olympics opening ceremony? The queen appeared in a mini *James Bond* movie directed by Danny Boyle. Actor Daniel Craig as James Bond is shown arriving at Buckingham Palace and accompanying Elizabeth (and her two corgis) into a helicopter. A helicopter then hovers over Olympic Park (later named Queen Elizabeth Olympic Park after the games) as two parachutists— one dressed in a copycat outfit to the queen—jump out and land on the field below as the theme of *James Bond* plays over the loudspeakers. A collective gasp can be heard from the crowd of sixty thousand (with a global TV audience of nearly one billion) in footage from the live event. Her Majesty then appears in the stands in the same outfit to roaring cheers from the crowd...okay, we totally get that they were stunt doubles, but we still have chills!

The queen had just one requirement before agreeing to the cameo. Angela Kelly, the queen's longtime dresser and close confidante, wrote in her authorized biography, *The Other Side of the Coin: The Queen, the Dresser and the Wardrobe*, that Elizabeth would only take part if she had a speaking part. "I asked whether she would like to say: 'Good evening, James,' or: 'Good evening, Mr. Bond,' and she chose the latter, knowing the Bond films," Kelly wrote. "Within minutes, I was back in [the queen's private press secretary] Edward's office delivering the good news to Danny [Boyle]—I think he almost fell off his chair when I said that the queen's only stipulation was that she could deliver that iconic line."

The year 2022 will mark the Queen's Platinum Jubilee, aka seventy years since she ascended the throne. Her coronation wasn't until June 2, 1953, due to the period of mourning after her father King George VI's death, so the jubilee will be celebrated on June 2, 2022 (though the celebrations will last all year).

Buckingham Palace announced a weekend of celebrations (and an extended bank holiday) from June 2 until June 5, 2022. The schedule includes Trooping the Colour (the annual parade for the queen's birthday), the lighting of Platinum Jubilee beacons, a Service of Thanksgiving at St. Paul's Cathedral, the Derby at Epsom Downs, a live concert called "Platinum Party at the Palace," the Big Jubilee Lunch, and the Platinum Jubilee Pageant.

The queen has worn the Imperial State Crown to every opening of Parliament since her reign began. Why did she stop wearing it in 2016?

It could be because she considers it "unwieldy," and we don't blame her. The Imperial State Crown, worn at the end of the queen's coronation and at the annual state openings of Parliament, weighs 2.3 pounds. The diamond-encrusted headpiece is set with a whopping 2868 diamonds, 17 sapphires, 11 emeralds, and 269 pearls, with the centerpiece being the 317-carat Cullinan II, the second largest stone cut from the Cullinan Diamond.

The queen hasn't worn the Imperial State Crown for the opening of Parliament since 2016, reportedly due to her advancing years and its heavy weight. In 2019 and 2021, the crown was carried in front of her as she made her way to her seat, and it was placed on a velvet cushion next to her as she gave the Queen's Speech (her annual address to formally open Parliament).

In the 2018 BBC documentary *The Coronation*, the queen talked about how she managed to continually honor tradition with the headpiece. Alastair Bruce, an expert on the Crown Jewels sat down with Her Majesty in the documentary. He said, "It's difficult to always remember that diamonds are stones and so they're very heavy." The queen replied: "Yes, fortunately, my father and I have about the same sort of shaped head. But once you put it on it stays. I mean it just remains on."

"You can't look down to read the speech, you have to take the speech up. Because if you did, your neck would break—it would fall off," she said with a smile. "So there are some disadvantages to crowns, but otherwise they're quite important things."

In the same documentary, St. Edward's Crown, the one used briefly during the coronation ceremony, is also brought out for Her Majesty to inspect. "Is it still as heavy? Yes, yes it is," the queen remarked, answering her own question, as she picked it up. "It weighs a ton." And she wasn't kidding: The crown contains 444 stones set on a solid-gold frame and weighs nearly five pounds (or the equivalent of about six cans of soup) and is also on public display at the Tower of London.

Prince Philip, Queen Elizabeth II's husband, died in April 2021. Why was it so significant that the queen sat alone at his funeral?

*I*t's an image that's seared into our collective memory: Her Majesty the Queen, dressed in a black coat and signature pearls, head bowed in a black wide-brim hat, face (and, possibly, tears) obscured by a matching mask, sitting solitary in the pew of St. George's Chapel to bid her husband of seventy-three years a final farewell. The profound image and its lonely (yet universal) message resonated with a nation—and world—in mourning after a year-long battle with the COVID-19 pandemic.

The Duke of Edinburgh passed away of "old age," according to his death certificate, on the morning of April 9, 2021, at Windsor Castle, aged ninety-nine, just two months before his one hundredth birthday. He had stayed in two hospitals in the weeks leading up to his death, the longest being sixteen days at St. Bartholomew's Hospital following a procedure for a preexisting heart condition. He was the longest-serving royal consort in British history.

The royal family immediately put out a statement saying, "It is with deep sorrow that Her Majesty The Queen announces the death of her beloved husband, His Royal Highness The

Prince Philip, Duke of Edinburgh. His Royal Highness passed away peacefully this morning at Windsor Castle." Members of the royal family changed their social media profile pictures to black-and-white monograms to signify the period of mourning, and politicians, celebrities, and royalty from around the world sent their condolences to Queen Elizabeth II upon his death.

The funeral, whose plans were nicknamed Operation Forth Bridge, took place on April 17, 2021. It was attended by only thirty guests due to COVID-19 restrictions, but the pared-back ceremony was actually something the no-fuss, no-frills Duke of Edinburgh might have wanted. The queen reportedly carried a few mementos of Philip's in her signature Launer handbag: a photograph of her with Philip in the early days of their marriage, believed to be taken in Malta, and a white silk handkerchief by Kent & Haste, known to be a favorite of the late Duke's.

Queen Elizabeth II was back to work in no time, though, resuming her royal duties just four days after Philip's death. She attended a retirement ceremony for the royal household's most senior official on April 13, and held virtual audiences with two ambassadors just ten days after the funeral on April 27. She continued her official engagements throughout the summer of 2021, then embarked on her annual summer holiday to Balmoral at the beginning of August.

FAMILY TREE

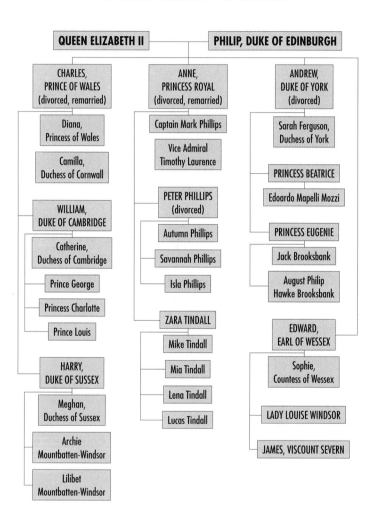

ROYAL TRIVIA

RESOURCES AND FURTHER READING

The Cambridges

Apple Jr., R. W. "Princess of Wales Has Boy: Charles Is 'Over the Moon.'" *The New York Times.* June 22, 1982. https://www.nytimes.com/1982/06/22/world/princess-of-wales-has-boy-charles-is-over-the-moon.html.

Armstrong, Lisa. "Exclusive: Carole Middleton's First Interview: 'Life Is Really Normal—Most of the Time." *The Telegraph.* November 30, 2018. https://www.telegraph.co.uk/women/life/exclusive-carole-middletons-first-interview-life-really-normal.

BBC. "That Prince William Episode." *That Peter Crouch Euros Pod.* Podcast Audio. July 29, 2020. https://www.bbc.co.uk/programmes/p08m3ckl/clips.

Bernstein, Fred. "William the Terrible." *People.* July 7, 1986. https://people.com/archive/cover-story-william-the-terrible-vol-26-no-1.

Bowie, Rachel and Roberta Fiorito. "Happy Anni, Kate & Wills! With Special Guests Myka Meier and Elizabeth Holmes." *Gallery Media Group: Royally Obsessed Podcast.* Podcast Audio. April 29, 2021. https://podcasts.apple.com/us/podcast/happy-anni-kate-wills-special-guests-myka-meier-elizabeth/id1365334446?i=1000519210465.

"COVID-19: Prince William 'Tested Positive in April." BBC. November 2, 2020. https://www.bbc.com/news/uk-54774942.

Dowd, Kathy Ehrich. "Kate Middleton—Oh So Lovely As Eliza Doolittle at Age 11." *People.* Last updated January 27, 2014. https://people.com/celebrity/kate-middleton-oh-so-lovely-as-eliza-doolittle-at-age-11.

Duke and Duchess of Cambridge. *Instagram.*

D'Zurilla, Christie. "Prince George Meets Bilby Namesake in Royal Visit to Taronga Zoo." *Los Angeles Times.* April 21, 2014. https://www.latimes.com/entertainment/gossip/la-et-mg-prince-george-taronga-zoo-bilby-australia-royal-visit-20140421-story.html.

Elston, Laura. "How the Duchess of Cambridge First Caught Prince William's Eye in Catwalk Show." *Evening Standard.* April 29, 2021.

https://www.standard.co.uk/news/uk/kate-middleton-prince-william-st-andrews-catwalk-show-b932076.html.

Fletcher, Giovanna. "The Duchess of Cambridge on the Early Years." *Happy Mum Happy Baby* Podcast. Podcast Audio. February 15, 2020. https://podcasts.apple.com/ca/podcast/the-duchess-of-cambridge-on-the-early-years/id1277078956?i=1000465682542.

Foussianes, Chloe. "Everything You Need to Know About Anmer Hall, Prince William and Kate Middleton's Country Home." *Town & Country*. July 1, 2020. https://www.townandcountrymag.com/style/home-decor/a25646036/anmer-hall-prince-william-kate-middleton-george-louis-princess-charlotte-country-home.

Foussianes, Chloe. "Kate Middleton's Favorite Celebrity That She's Met Is...David Attenborough." *Town & Country*. April 10, 2020. https://www.townandcountrymag.com/society/tradition/a32105884/kate-middleton-david-attenborough-favorite-celebrity.

Frangoul, Anmar. "Prince William Launches £50 Million Earthshot Prize, with a Nod to John F. Kennedy." CNBC. Last updated October 8, 2020. https://www.cnbc.com/2020/10/08/prince-william-launches-50-million-earthshot-prize.html.

Gething, Ashley, dir. *Diana, Our Mother: Her Life and Legacy*. United Kingdom: HBO, 2017.

Glauber, Bill. "Prince William at School: Just Another Eton Boy?" *The Baltimore Sun*. September 5, 1995. https://www.baltimoresun.com/news/bs-xpm-1995-09-05-1995248083-story.html.

Gonzales, Erica. "The Queen Honors Kate Middleton with a High Rank in Chivalry." *Harper's Bazaar*. June 3, 2019. https://www.harpersbazaar.com/celebrity/latest/a27308936/queen-gives-kate-middleton-royal-victorian-order.

Green, Jessica. "Prince William's Bolognese Sauce: Duke of Cambridge Shares Recipe for Classic Italian Dish He Used to 'Impress' Kate Middleton..." *Daily Mail*. Last updated October 31, 2020. https://www.dailymail.co.uk/femail/article-8892203/Prince-William-shares-recipe-homemade-Bolognese-sauce.html.

Greenspan, Rachel. "Why Prince Harry and Meghan Markle Are Leaving the Charity They Started with Prince William and Kate Middleton." *Time*. June 20, 2019. https://time.com/5611130/harry-meghan-leaving-royal-foundation.

Hallemann, Caroline. "Kate Middleton Publishes a Photographer Book." *Town & Country*. May 7, 2021. https://www.townandcountrymag.com/society/tradition/a35960777/kate-middleton-hold-still-covid-photography-book.

"Highlights from Prince William and Kate Middleton's 2011 Tour of Canada." *Hello! Magazine*. Accessed July 8, 2021. https://www.hellomagazine.com/royalty/gallery/2016072869266/prince-william-kate-middleton-highlights-tour-canada-2011/1.

Hills, Megan C. "Kate Middleton Asked for a Part-Time Job Due to Her 'Relationship With This Very High Profile Man' According to Royal Expert." *Evening Standard*. June 12, 2020. https://www.standard.co.uk/insider/royals/kate-middleton-asked-for-a-part-time-job-due-to-her-relationship-with-this-very-high-profile-man-a4466731.html.

Hills, Megan C. "Mustique Villa Antilles: Inside Kate Middleton and Prince William's Lavish £56K Summer Holiday Villa." *Evening Standard*. July 31, 2019. https://www.standard.co.uk/insider/living/mustique-villa-antilles-inside-kate-middleton-and-prince-william-s-lavish-ps56k-summer-holiday-villa-a4202711.html.

Holmes, Elizabeth. *HRH: So Many Thoughts on Royal Style*. New York: Celadon Books, 2020.

Holt, Bethan. *The Duchess of Cambridge: A Decade of Modern Royal Style*. London: Ryland, Peters & Small. 2021.

Hunt, Peter. "The Royal Wedding: Who Pays the Bill?" *BBC America*. April 29, 2011. https://www.bbcamerica.com/anglophenia/2011/01/the-royal-wedding-who-pays-the-bill.

Hurtado, Alexandra. "Why William and Kate Broke Up in 2007—and Why They Got Back Together." *Parade Magazine*. January 3, 2021. https://parade.com/152491/alexandra-hurtado/why-william-and-kate-broke-up-in-2007-and-why-they-got-back-together.

ITV News. "In Full: William and Kate's 2010 Engagement Interview." YouTube Video. November 16, 2020. https://www.youtube.com/watch?v=2hPi38x90ks.

Kantrowitz, Barbara. "Prince Charming." *Newsweek*. June 25, 2000. https://www.newsweek.com/prince-charming-160863.

Kindelan, Katie and Carolyn Durand. "Prince William, Princess Kate Make Prince Louis's Birth Official." *Good Morning America*. May 1, 2018. https://www.goodmorningamerica.com/culture/story/prince-william-princess-kate-make-prince-louiss-birth-54848871.

Kim, Susanna. "Royal Wedding: Kate Middleton's Family Chips In But Security Most Costly." *ABC News*. April 28, 2011. https://abcnews.go.com/Business/

Royal_Wedding/royal-wedding-costs-kate-middletons-family-chips-security/story?id=13480159.

Krueger, Alyson. "The Making of a Modern Queen." *People*. June 4, 2021.

Langfitt, Frank. "Princess Diana Statue Unveiling Shows Mixed Emotions Over Role of Princes Her Sons." NPR. July 4, 2021. https://www.npr.org/2021/07/04/1012978346/princess-diana-statue-unveiling-shows-mixed-emotions-over-role-of-princes-her-so.

Leasca, Stacey. "We Just Got a Glimpse of Kate Middleton's Most-Used Emojis." *Travel & Leisure*. December 2, 2020. https://www.travelandleisure.com/travel-tips/celebrity-travel/kate-middleton-emojis.

Lyall, Sarah. "Duchess of Cambridge Gives Birth to a Baby Boy." *The New York Times*. July 22, 2013. https://www.nytimes.com/2013/07/23/world/europe/royal-baby.html.

MacKelden, Amy. "See Inside Duchess Kate and Prince William's Vacation Villa in Mustique." *Harper's Bazaar*. August 3, 2019. https://www.harpersbazaar.com/celebrity/latest/a28591974/kate-middleton-prince-william-mustique-villa-photos.

Maloney, Maggie. "8 Surprising Things You Might Not Know About Kate Middleton's Wedding Dress." *Town & Country*. April 20, 2021. https://www.townandcountrymag.com/the-scene/weddings/a20517182/kate-middleton-wedding-dress.

Miller, Julie. "How Prince William and Kate Middleton Paid Tribute to Princess Diana on Their Wedding Day." *Vanity Fair*. April 25, 2018. https://www.vanityfair.com/style/2018/04/prince-william-kate-middleton-royal-wedding-princess-diana.

Morton, Andrew. *Diana: Her True Story in Her Own Words*. New York: Pocket Books, 1998.

"New Rules on Royal Succession Come Into Force." BBC. March 26, 2015. https://www.bbc.com/news/uk-32073399.

Nicholl, Katie. "Wills and the Real Girl." *Vanity Fair*. November 4, 2010. https://www.vanityfair.com/news/2010/12/william-and-kate-201012.

O'Malley, Katie. "Kate Middleton's Blue Engagement Dress May Have Triggered the Downfall for Fashion Brand Issa." *Elle*. February 27, 2017. https://www.elle.com/uk/fashion/celebrity-style/news/a34185/kate-middleton-blue-issa-engagement-dress-daniella-helayel.

Pasquini, Maria and Simon Perry. "Prince William and Kate Middleton Adopted New Puppy Before Death of Family Dog Lupo." *People*. 2021. https://people.com/royals/prince-william-kate-middleton-adopted-new-puppy-before-death-family-dog-lupo.

Pearl, Diana. "Ellie Goulding Recalls Singing for Prince William and Kate on Their Wedding Day: 'My Hands Were Shaking.'" *People.* Last updated February 26, 2016. https://people.com/royals/ellie-goulding-was-nervous-to-sing-at-prince-william-kates-royal-wedding.

Peltier, Elian. "Prince William Announces New Prize Aimed at 'Repairing' the Planet." *The New York Times.* Last updated March 11, 2021. https://www.nytimes.com/2020/10/08/world/europe/prince-william-environment-earthshot-prize.html.

"Royal Baby: Duchess of Cambridge Gives Birth to Daughter." BBC. May 2, 2015. https://www.bbc.com/news/uk-32562117.

Sacks, Rebecca. "Anglesey in Photos: Kate and William's Storybook Welsh Island." *Vanity Fair.* September 29, 2014. https://www.vanityfair.com/style/photos/2011/06/prince-william-kate-middleton-anglesey-slide-show-201106.

Saunders, Nicole. "Kate Middleton's Stylist Natasha Archer Receives an Impressive Royal Honor." *Harper's BAZAAR.* May 3, 2019. https://www.harpersbazaar.com/celebrity/latest/a27355618/kate-middleton-stylist-natasha-archer-royal-victorian-order.

Sher, Lauren. "Royal Wedding: Prince William and Catherine Middleton Kiss Twice on Balcony As World Watches." *ABC News.* April 28, 2011. https://abcnews.go.com/International/Royal_Wedding/royal-wedding-prince-william-kate-middletons-balcony-kiss/story?id=13480895.

Strong, Gemma. "Royals Who Are Left-Handed: From Prince William to Sophie Wessex." *Hello! Magazine.* August 13, 2020. https://www.hellomagazine.com/royalty/2020081395315/british-royals-left-handed.

The Royal Family. "Duchess of Cambridge Reveals the Results of Her 5 Big Questions Survey." The Royal Household. https://www.royal.uk/5BigInsights.

The Royal Family. "The Wedding of Prince William and Catherine Middleton." YouTube Video. April 29, 2011. https://www.youtube.com/watch?v=schQZY3QjCw.

Thomas, Jo. "The Early Education of a Future King. *The New York Times.* April 13, 1986. https://www.nytimes.com/1986/04/13/education/the-early-education-of-a-future-king.html.

Vanderhoof, Erin. "How Kate Middleton and Prince William's Wedding Ushered in the Modern-Day Royal Media Obsession." *Vanity Fair.* April 29, 2021. https://www.vanityfair.com/style/2021/04/kate-middleton-and-prince-william-wedding-royal-media-obsession.

"William and Kate's Royal Visit to North America." *Today Show*. Last updated July 1, 2011. https://www.today.com/slideshow/william-and-kates-royal-visit-to-north-america-43605076.

Williams, Martin, dir. *Prince William: A Planet For Us All*. United Kingdom: Oxford Films, 2020.

Williams, Rhiannon. "First Look Inside the Duke and Duchess of Cambridge's Anglesey Home." *The Telegraph*. September 23, 2014. https://www.tele graph.co.uk/news/uknews/prince-william/10328491/First-look-inside-the-Duke-and-Duchess-of-Cambridges-Anglesey-home.html.

Wilson, Eric. "Bride's Dress Is a Flawless Success." *The New York Times*. April 29, 2011. https://www.nytimes.com/2011/04/30/fashion/weddings/30royaldress.html

The Sussexes

"Archewell: Compassion in Action." *Archewell*. https://archewell.com.

"Archewell Productions Announces First Netflix Series, In Partnership With The Invictus Games Foundation." *Netflix*. April 6, 2021. https://about.netflix.com/en/news/archewell-productions-announces-first-netflix-series-in-partnership-with-the.

Barbour, Shannon. "Meghan Markle's 'The Tig' Blog Is a Treasure Trove of Information About Her Personal Life." *Cosmopolitan*. April 21, 2020. https://www.cosmopolitan.com/entertainment/a20145547/meghan-markle-lifestyle-blog-tig-facts-photos.

BBC News. "FULL Interview: Prince Harry and Meghan Markle - BBC News." YouTube Video. November 27, 2017. https://www.youtube.com/watch?v=LQicq60aJaw.

Boswell, Josh and Ryan Parry. "David Foster Arranged Harry and Meghan's Canadian 'Getaway'." *The Daily Mail*. Last updated January 8, 2020 https://www.dailymail.co.uk/news/article-7846385/David-Foster-arranged-Harry-Meghans-stay-mystery-millionaires-Canadian-mansion.html.

Boucher, Ashley "Meghan Markle and Prince Harry Have Bought a House & 'Settled into the Quiet Privacy' of Santa Barbara." *People*. August 11, 2020. https://people.com/royals/meghan-markle-and-prince-harry-bought-a-house-in-santa-barbara.

Durand, Carolyn and Omid Scobie. *Finding Freedom*. New York: Dey Street Books, 2020.

Edmonds, Lizzie. "The Me You Can't See: Key Moments from Prince Harry's Docuseries." Evening Standard. May 26, 2021. https://www.standard.co

.uk/news/world/the-me-you-cant-see-prince-harry-oprah-interview-key-moments-apple-b936458.html.

Foussianes, Chloe. "How Prince Harry Served in Afghanistan in Secret-Despite the Notoriously Cutthroat U.K. Press." *Town & Country*. April 19, 2019. https://www.townandcountrymag.com/society/tradition/a27205954/prince-harry-afghanistan-media-blackout.

Furness, Hannah. "Revealed: Prince Harry and Meghan Plan Non-profit Empire under the Name Archewell, 'to Do Something of Meaning.'" *The Telegraph*. April 6, 2020. https://www.telegraph.co.uk/royal-family/2020/04/06/revealed-prince-harry-meghan-plan-non-profit-empire-name-archewell.

Gething, Ashley, dir. *Diana, Our Mother: Her Life and Legacy*. London, United Kingdom: ITV, Oxford Film & Television, HBO, 2017.

Goldberg, Carrie. "Everything We Know About Meghan Markle's Wedding Gown." *Harper's Bazaar*. May 19, 2018. https://www.harpersbazaar.com/wedding/photos/a13938657/meghan-markle-wedding-dress.

Goodey, Emma. "The Duke of Sussex." The Royal Family. May 21, 2020. https://www.royal.uk/The-Duke-of-Sussex.

Guerrera, Antonello, Stefanie Bolzen, Arnaud De la Grange, and Rafa de Miguel. "Justin Welby: What I Learnt from Covid, the Threat of Cancel Culture and the Truth on Harry & Meghan's Wedding." *La Repubblica*. March 31, 2021. https://www.repubblica.it/esteri/2021/03/30/news/justin_welby_what_i_learnt_from_covid_the_threat_of_cancel_culture_and_the_truth_on_harry_meghan_s_wedding_-294433010.

Hallemann, Caroline. "Archie Harrison Was Christened Today in the Private Chapel at Windsor Castle." *Town & Country*. July 6, 2019. https://www.townandcountrymag.com/society/tradition/a27919631/archie-harrison-christening-details.

"Harry's a Real Hit with Spice Girls." *BBC News*. November 2, 1997. http://news.bbc.co.uk/2/hi/19914.stm.

Hill, Erin. "Princess Meghan! Meghan Markle's Official Occupation Revealed on Baby Archie's Birth Certificate." *People*. May 17, 2019. https://people.com/royals/meghan-markle-official-occupation-princess-united-kingdom-baby-archie-birth-certificate.

Hill, Matt, dir. *Queen of the World*. London, United Kingdom: Oxford Films, ITV, HBO, 2018.

Hill, Sarah, prod. *The Forgotten Kingdom: Prince Harry in Lesotho*. London, United Kingdom: ITN, ITV1, 2004.

Inside Edition. "See Meghan Markle on '90s Nickelodeon Show After Protesting Commercial" YouTube Video, 2:17. November 30, 2017. https://www.youtube.com/watch?v=tfaGleA4qYo.

Kapadia, Asif and Dawn Porter, dirs. *The Me You Can't See*. United States: Apple TV+, 2021.

Kashner, Sam. "Cover Story: Meghan Markle, Wild About Harry!" *Vanity Fair*. September 6, 2017. https://www.vanityfair.com/style/2017/09/meghan-markle-cover-story.

Kyo, Grace Alyssa, and Hannah Roche. "What Happened during Meghan Markle's First Marriage?" *Grazia*. November 30, 2017. https://graziamagazine.com/articles/happened-meghan-markles-first-marriage.

Landler, Mark. "U.K. Tabloid Invaded Meghan's Privacy, Judge Says." *The New York Times*. Last updated February 17, 2021. https://www.nytimes.com/2021/02/11/world/europe/meghan-markle-privacy-mail-on-sunday.html.

The Late Late Show with James Corden. "An Afternoon with Prince Harry & James Corden." YouTube Video. February 25, 2021. https://www.youtube.com/watch?v=7oxlCKMlpZw.

Levin, Angela. "Exclusive: Prince Harry on Chaos after Diana's Death and Why the World Needs "the Magic" of the Royal Family." *Newsweek*. May 18, 2018. https://www.newsweek.com/2017/06/30/prince-harry-depression-diana-death-why-world-needs-magic-627833.html.

Lippiett, Nathan, dir. *Harry & Meghan: An African Journey*. London, United Kingdom: ITN Productions, ITV, 2019.

Magra, Iliana, and Daniel Victor. "Prince Harry and Meghan Markle Announce She's Pregnant." *The New York Times*. October 15, 2018. https://www.nytimes.com/2018/10/15/world/europe/meghan-markle-prince-harry-pregnant.html.

Malkin, Russ, dir. *Prince Harry in Africa*. London, United Kingdom: Big Earth Productions, 2016.

Markle, Meghan. "Farewell, Darling." *The Tig*. April 7, 2017. http://thetig.com.

Markle, Meghan. "Meghan Markle: I'm More Than An 'Other'." *ELLE*. March 10, 2021. https://www.elle.com/uk/life-and-culture/news/a26855/more-than-an-other/.

Markle, Meghan. "Meghan, The Duchess of Sussex: My Conversation with Gloria Steinem." *Yahoo!* August 26, 2020. https://www.yahoo.com/now/meghan-the-duchess-of-sussex-my-conversation-with-gloria-steinem-151902708.html.

Markle, Meghan. "The Losses We Share." *The New York Times*. November 25, 2020. https://www.nytimes.com/2020/11/25/opinion/meghan-markle-miscarriage.html.

Matousek, Mark. "Resurfaced Video Shows a Young Meghan Markle Asking Procter & Gamble to Change a Commercial with Sexist Undertones." *Business Insider*. December 01, 2017. https://www.businessinsider.com/meghan-markle-spoke-out-about-commercial-2017-11.

"Meghan Markle." *IMDb*. https://www.imdb.com/name/nm1620783.

Morton, Andrew. *Meghan: A Hollywood Princess*. New York: Grand Central Publishing, 2018.

Perry, Simon and Stephanie Petit. "The Queen's 'Some Recollections May Vary' Statement Was 'Underlying Jab' at Meghan and Harry's Interview." *People*. March 18, 2021. https://people.com/royals/queens-some-recollections-may-vary-statement-was-underlying-jab-at-harry-and-meghans-interview.

"Princess Di Gives Birth to Boy." *Associated Press*. September 16, 1984. https://news.google.com/newspapers?id=V19GAAAAIBAJ&pg=1677,1656508&dq=princess+diana&hl=en.

Puente, Maria. "Prince Harry Accepts Apology, Libel Damages from Tabloid in Latest Legal Victory over Media." *USA Today*. Last updated February 1, 2021. https://www.usatoday.com/story/entertainment/celebrities/2020/12/28/prince-harry-gets-correction-apology-tabloid-over-military-story/4063034001/

Shepard, Dax and Monica Padman. "Prince Harry." Armchair Expert Podcast. Podcast Audio. May 13, 2021. https://open.spotify.com/episode/476cnLBpxWp2HgsqfiAtBe?si=kycc49s2Q02AzTQLPud6sQ&dl_branch=1.

VanHoose, Benjamin. "Princess Diana Announced Her Second Pregnancy on Valentine's Day, Just Like Meghan Markle and Prince Harry." *People*. February 14, 2021. https://people.com/royals/princess-diana-valentines-day-pregnancy-announcement-just-like-prince-harry-meghan-markle.

Winfrey, Oprah. "Oprah with Meghan and Harry: A CBS Primetime Special." CBS. March 8, 2021.

Princess Diana

Anne Hughes, Sarah. "Katie Couric Talks to Princes William and Harry About Queen Elizabeth, Having Kids." *Washington Post*. May 30, 2012. https://www.washingtonpost.com/blogs/celebritology/post/

katie-couric-talks-to-princes-william-and-harry-about-queen-elizabeth-having-kids/2012/05/30/gJQAjnur1U_blog.html.

Apple Jr., R. W. "Amid Splendor, Charles Weds Diana." *The New York Times*. July 30, 1981. https://www.nytimes.com/1981/07/30/world/amid-splendor-charles-weds-diana.html.

Barcelona, Ainhoa. "Princess Diana's Sweet Childhood Nickname Revealed in Resurfaced Letter." *Hello!* September 3, 2018. https://www.hellomagazine.com/royalty/2018090361835/princess-diana-sweet-childhood-nickname.

Barr, Sabrina. "Who Was Raine Spencer? The Story of the Socialite Who Became Princess Diana's Stepmother." *The Independent*. February 22, 2020. https://www.independent.co.uk/life-style/royal-family/princess-diana-stepmother-raine-spencer-royal-family-documentary-channel-4-a9347226.html.

Bashir, Martin. "The Panorama Interview." London, United Kingdom: BBC1 Panorama. November 20, 1995. http://www.bbc.co.uk/news/special/politics97/diana/panorama.html.

Bickerstaff, Isaac. "Tatler Dynasties: Meet the Spencers." *Tatler*. April 26, 2021. https://www.tatler.com/gallery/the-spencer-family-princess-diana

Borders, William. "Prince Charles to Wed 19-Year-Old Family Friend." *The New York Times*. February 25, 1981. https://www.nytimes.com/1981/02/25/world/prince-charles-to-wed-19-year-old-family-friend.html.

Brown, Tina. *The Diana Chronicles*. New York: Random House, 2007.

Butan, Christina. "See the Moment Princess Diana Introduced Prince William to the World 36 Years Ago Today." *People.* June 21, 2018. https://people.com/royals/princess-diana-prince-william-birth.

Cantrell, Liz. "Princess Diana's Older Sister Lady Sarah McCorquodale Once Dated Prince Charles." *Town & Country*. November 15, 2020. https://www.townandcountrymag.com/society/tradition/a34288939/princess-diana-sister-lady-sarah-mccorquodale.

Collins, Nancy. "Sarah Ferguson: Diana, the Queen and I." *Harper's Bazaar*. October 12, 2018. https://www.harpersbazaar.com/celebrity/latest/news/a730/sarah-ferguson-divorce-interview.

Conti, Samantha. "Elizabeth Emanuel Talks Princess Diana's Wedding Gown, New Beginnings." *WWD.* June 2, 2021. https://wwd.com/fashion-news/fashion-features/elizabeth-emanuel-talks-princess-dianas-wedding-gown-new-beginnings-1234834263.

Gamarekian, Barbara. "On the Menu: Champagne, Dancing and Manners." *The New York Times*. November 10, 1985. https://www.nytimes.com/1985/11/10/us/on-the-menu-champagne-dancing-andmanners.html.

Goldberg, Melissa. "Yes, Princess Diana Actually Picked Out Her Iconic Engagement Ring." *Oprah Daily*. November 16, 2020. https://www.oprahdaily.com/entertainment/a34437384/princess-diana-engagement-ring.

Gregory, Alice. "Lessons from the Last Swiss Finishing School." *The New Yorker*. October 8, 2018. https://www.newyorker.com/magazine/2018/10/08/lessons-from-the-last-swiss-finishing-school.

Hill, Erin. "All About Princess Diana's Wedding Day Perfume—and How It Actually Spilled on Her Dress!" *People*. July 29, 2018. https://people.com/royals/princess-dianas-wedding-day-perfume.

Hines, Ree. "John Travolta Recalls 'Magical Moment' He Asked Princess Diana to Ask." *Today*. April 22, 2021. https://www.today.com/popculture/john-travolta-recalls-dancing-princess-diana-t215946.

Holmes, Elizabeth. *HRH: So Many Thoughts on Royal Style*. New York: Celadon Books, 2020.

iLovePrincessDiana. "Princess Diana's Engagement Interview." YouTube Video. December 11, 2010. https://www.youtube.com/watch?v=wg_fib2gQaU

Ivie, Devon. "Princess Diana's Dance Partner Remembers Their Dazzling 'Uptown Girl' Performance." *Vulture*. November 18, 2020. https://www.vulture.com/article/the-crown-princess-diana-uptown-girl-dance-wayne-sleep-interview.html.

Kiernan, Louise. "Job Afforded Diana a 'Normal Life.'" *Chicago Tribune*. September 5, 1997. https://www.chicagotribune.com/news/ct-xpm-1997-09-05-9709050308-story.html.

Knight, Sam. "The Power and Paranoia of the BBC's Princess Diana Interview." *The New Yorker*. May 27, 2021. https://www.newyorker.com/news/daily-comment/the-power-and-paranoia-of-the-diana-interview.

Kranc, Lauren. "Prince Charles and Princess Diana's 1983 Australia Tour Marked the Fracturing of Their Relationship." *Esquire*. November 26, 2020. https://www.esquire.com/entertainment/tv/a34761395/prince-charles-princess-diana-1983-australia-tour-the-crown.

Kyung Kim, Eun. "Princess Diana's Youngest Bridesmaid Shares Memories from THAT Royal Wedding." *Today*. April 19, 2018. https://www.today.com/news/princess-diana-s-bridesmaid-clementine-hambro-shares-royal-wedding-memories-t127169

Maloney, Maggie. "The 26 Most Gorgeous Royal Wedding Tiara Moments
of All Time." *Town & Country*. July 18, 2020. https://www.townandcountry
mag.com/the-scene/weddings/g17805394/royal-wedding-tiaras-
throughout-history.

Morton, Andrew. *Diana: Her True Story*. New York: Pocket Books, 1992.

Morton, Andrew. *Diana: Her True Story in Her Own Words*. New York: Pocket
Books, 1998.

Newbold, Alice. "The Story Behind Princess Diana's 'Amazing, Completely
OTT' Wedding Dress." *Vogue UK*. September 7, 2020. https://www.vogue
.co.uk/fashion/article/princess-diana-wedding-dress.

Pearce Rotondi, Jessica. "How Prince Charles and Lady Diana's Wedding
Became a Global Phenomenon." *History*. December 2, 2020. https://www
.history.com/news/prince-charles-lady-diana-wedding.

Petit, Stephanie. "The Real Story of Princess Diana's 'Revenge' Dress—and
How She Nearly Didn't Wear It." *People.* July 7, 2020. https://people.com/
royals/princess-diana-revenge-dress-true-story.

Picheta, Rob. "Princess Diana to Receive Plaque Outside the London Flat
She Lived in Before Marrying Charles." *CNN*. Last updated April 1, 2021.
https://www.cnn.com/style/article/princess-diana-london-blue-plaque-
scli-gbr-intl/index.html.

Puckett-Pope, Lauren. "Prince Charles and Camilla's 'Fred' and 'Gladys'
Nicknames Were Inspired by a Comedy Show." *Harper's Bazaar*. November
16, 2020. https://www.harpersbazaar.com/culture/film-tv/a34691124/
prince-charles-camilla-parker-bowles-fred-gladys.

Robinson, Katie. "The Untold Story Behind Kate Middleton's Engagement Ring."
Town & Country. March 24, 2021. https://www.townandcountrymag.com/
style/jewelry-and-watches/a13052347/kate-middleton-engagement-ring.

Scott, Caroline. "Charles Spencer and His Wife, Karen, on Diana, Childhood
Trauma and Finding Happiness." *The Sunday Times*. September 13, 2020.
https://www.thetimes.co.uk/article/charles-spencer-and-his-wife-karen-
on-diana-childhood-trauma-and-finding-happiness-h3qrr6fn2.

Spranklen, Annabelle. "The Real Story of How Prince Charles Fell for Lady
Diana Spencer." *Tatler*. May 6, 2021. https://www.tatler.com/article/
prince-charles-and-princess-diana-relationship.

Spranklen, Annabelle. "The Sweet Nod Princess Diana Made to Her
Family with Her Choice of Wedding Tiara." *Tatler*. August 11, 2020.
https://www.tatler.com/article/princess-diana-wedding-tiara.

Syme, Rachel. "The Second Life of Princess Diana's Most Notorious Sweater."
The New Yorker. November 20, 2020. https://www.newyorker.com/

culture/on-and-off-the-avenue/the-second-life-of-princess-dianas-most-iconic-sweater.

Taylor, Elise. "*The Crown*: What Really Happened During Princess Diana and Prince Charles's Fateful Tour of Australia." *Vogue*. November 15, 2020. https://www.vogue.com/article/princess-diana-and-prince-charles-fateful-tour-of-australia.

Telegraph Reporters. "Princess Diana: What Happened on the Night of Her Death?" *The Telegraph*. August 29, 2017. https://www.telegraph.co.uk/royal-family/0/princess-diana-happened-night-death.

Thames TV "Royal Wedding: Princess Diana and Prince Charles." YouTube Video. February 12, 2017. https://www.youtube.com/watch?v=lXhGswv7wdc.

Vincenty, Samantha. "How Princess Diana Changed the Way We Think About AIDS." *Oprah Daily*. November 27, 2020. https://www.oprahdaily.com/entertainment/tv-movies/a34550472/princess-diana-aids-charity-work.

Ward, Victoria. "A 'Lovely Coincidence': How Diana's Memory Is Brought Back By This Valentine's Day Baby News for Harry and Meghan." *The Telegraph*. February 14, 2021. https://www.telegraph.co.uk/news/2021/02/14/lovely-coincidence-dianas-memory-brought-back-valentines-day.

Waxman, Olivia B. "What to Know About the Royal Blood in Diana's Family." *Time*. August 30, 2017. https://time.com/4913806/princess-diana-anniversary-family-history.

Weaver, Hilary. "Princess Diana Detailed Her Memorable Meetings with Grace Kelly and Elizabeth Taylor." *Vanity Fair*. June 15, 2017. https://www.vanityfair.com/style/2017/06/princess-diana-detailed-encounters-with-elizabeth-taylor-and-grace-kelly.

Prince Charles

"70 Facts about HRH The Prince of Wales." *The Prince of Wales and The Duchess of Cornwall*. November 12, 2018. https://www.princeofwales.gov.uk/70-facts-about-hrh-prince-wales.

"After a Star-Crossed Romance, Prince Charles Will Get Married." *The New York Times*. February 10, 2005. https://www.nytimes.com/2005/02/10/international/europe/after-a-starcrossed-romance-prince-charles-will-get.html.

Associated Press. "Charles Exonerated in Avalanche Death : But Swiss Find His 6-Member Ski Group Collectively Caused Slide." *Los Angeles Times*. June 27, 1988. https://www.latimes.com/archives/la-xpm-1988-06-27-mn-3813-story.html.

Booth, Hannah. "Dr. Tedi Millward, at the First Welsh Language Protest, Aberystwyth, 2 February 1963." *The Guardian.* October 30, 2015. https://www.theguardian.com/artanddesign/2015/oct/30/dr-tedi-millward-welsh-language-protest-aberystwyth.

Bradford, Sarah. *Diana: Finally, the Complete Story.* New York: Penguin Books, 2007.

Bridcut, John, dir. *Prince, Son and Heir: Charles at 70.* London, United Kingdom: Crux Productions, BBC One, 2018.

Cassidy, Suzanne. "A Prince's Storybook Is Adapted to Television." *The New York Times.* November 5, 1991. https://www.nytimes.com/1991/11/05/movies/a-prince-s-storybook-is-adapted-to-television.html.

Clay, Charlie, dir. *Prince Charles: Inside the Duchy of Cornwall.* London, United Kingdom: BBC Studios' Unscripted Productions, ITV One, 2019.

Darnton, John. "Prince Charles, in TV Documentary, Admits to Infidelity." *The New York Times.* June 30, 1994. https://www.nytimes.com/1994/06/30/world/prince-charles-in-tv-documentary-admits-to-infidelity.html.

Dear, Paula. "Fans 'Panic Buy' 8 April Mementos." *BBC News.* Last updated April 05, 2005. http://news.bbc.co.uk/2/hi/uk_news/4412347.stm.

Dimbleby, Jonathan. *The Prince of Wales: A Biography.* New York: William Morrow & Co., 1994.

Ducas, Annoushka. "Interview with Lady Anne Glenconner." *My Life in Seven Charms.* Podcast Audio. October 22, 2020. https://podcasts.apple.com/gb/podcast/my-life-in-seven-charms-with-lady-anne-glenconner/id1535104132?i=1000495702862.

Harris, Carolyn. "Charles, The Prince of Wales's 1969 Investiture at Caernarfon Castle, 50 Years on." *History Extra.* November 18, 2019. https://www.historyextra.com/period/20th-century/charles-prince-wales-investiture-caernarfon-castle-50-years-welsh-nationalism-what-happened.

Harris, Katie and Daniel Smith, dirs. *The Royal Family at War.* London, United Kingdom: ITN Productions, Channel 5, 2019.

Hassall, John. "Prince Charles's Invitation to the Coronation, 1953." *Royal Collection Trust.* https://www.rct.uk/collection/themes/exhibitions/hrh-the-prince-of-wales-an-exhibition-to-celebrate-his-sixtieth-birthday/windsor-castle-drawings-gallery/prince-charless-invitation-to-the-coronation-1953.

HRH The Prince of Wales. *The Old Man of Lochnagar.* London, United Kingdom: Hamish Hamilton, 1980.

HRH The Prince of Wales. "With the Prince's Trust, we know we can make a crucial difference in these uncertain times." *The Telegraph*. September 26, 2020. https://www.telegraph.co.uk/news/2020/09/26/princes-trust-know-can-make-crucial-difference-uncertain-times.

Junor, Penny. *The Duchess: Camilla Parker Bowles and the Love Affair That Rocked the Crown*. New York: Harper Collins, 2018.

Junor, Penny. *The Firm: The Troubled Life of the House of Windsor*. New York: Harper Collins, 2006.

Mackelden, Amy. "Princess Diana & Prince Charles's Whirlwind Romance Ended in Tragedy." *Harper's Bazaar*. November 14, 2020. https://www.harpersbazaar.com/celebrity/latest/a34647773/princess-diana-prince-charles-relationship-timeline.

Martin, Christopher, dir. *Charles: The Private Man, The Public Role*. London, United Kingdom: Dimbleby Martin Productions, 1994.

"Prince Charles and Camilla Parker Bowles Marry." *The New York Times*. April 09, 2005. https://www.nytimes.com/2005/04/09/international/europe/prince-charles-and-camilla-parker-bowles-marry.html.

"Prince Charles through the Years, in Pictures." *The Telegraph*. November 15, 2020. https://www.telegraph.co.uk/royal-family/0/prince-charles-pictures-wales-best-photos-young/prince-wales-baby-birth-buckingham-palace-november-14-1948-announced/.

"Prince in Fatal Ski Incident." *The Guardian*. March 11, 1988. https://www.theguardian.com/uk/1988/mar/11/monarchy.fromthearchive.

Smith, Sally Bedell. "The Lonely Heir: Inside the Isolating Boarding School Days of Prince Charles." *Vanity Fair*. March 28, 2017. https://www.vanityfair.com/style/2017/03/the-isolating-boarding-school-days-of-prince-charles.

Smith, Sally Bedell. *Prince Charles: The Passions and Paradoxes of an Improbable Life*. New York: Random House, 2017.

Vallance, Adam. "Royal Residences: Clarence House." *The Royal Family*. January 05, 2017. https://www.royal.uk/royal-residences-clarence-house.

Queen Elizabeth II

Bruce, Christopher, dir. *The Queen at War*. New York, NY: PBS, ITV, BBC, 2020.

Carr, Flora. "The Real Friendship Between Queen Elizabeth and Billy Graham." *Time*. February 21, 2018. https://time.com/5168217/queen-billy-graham-friendship.

Cawston, Richard, dir. *Royal Family*. London, United Kingdom: BBC, ITV Productions, 1969.

Crawford, Marion. *The Little Princesses: The Story of the Queen's Childhood by Her Nanny, Marion Crawford*. New York: St. Martin's Griffin, 2003.

Dennison, Matthew. *The Queen*. London: Head of Zeus, 2021.

Dibdin, Emma and Michael Stillwell. "The British Royal Family Tree." *Town & Country*. April 12, 2021. https://www.townandcountrymag.com/society/a20736482/british-royal-family-tree.

Dilks, David. "The Queen and Mr. Churchill." International Churchill Society. June 29, 2013. https://winstonchurchill.org/publications/finest-hour/finest-hour-135/the-queen-and-mr-churchill.

Eade, Philip. *Prince Philip: The Turbulent Early Life of the Man Who Married Queen Elizabeth II*. New York: St. Martin's Griffin, 2012.

Gething, Ashley, dir. *Our Queen at 90*. London, United Kingdom: Oxford Film & Television, 2016.

Gold, Mick, dir. *Elizabeth: Our Queen*. London, United Kingdom: ITN Productions, CBC, 2018.

Goodey, Emma. "Her Majesty The Queen." The Royal Family. April 22, 2021. https://www.royal.uk/her-majesty-the-queen.

Harper, Zach. "The Queen Had Just One Request for Her James Bond Cameo during the 2012 London Olympics." *Hello! Canada*. November 6, 2019. https://ca.hellomagazine.com/royalty/02019103053528/queen-james-bond-cameo-2012-london-olympics-angela-kelly.

Higginson, Lucy. "16 of The Queen's Favourite Horses." *Horse & Hound*. June 9, 2016. https://www.horseandhound.co.uk/features/15-of-the-queens-favourite-horses-482896.

Holland, Brynn. "Watching *The Crown*? Here Are the Real Facts You Need to Know." *History*. Last updated December 22, 2020. https://www.history.com/news/history-behind-the-crown-queen-elizabeth-edward-margaret-fact-check.

Howard, Alathea Fitzalan. *The Windsor Diaries: My Childhood with the Princesses Elizabeth and Margaret*. New York: Atria Books, 2021.

Jackson, Chris. *Modern Monarchy: The British Royal Family Today*. New York: Rizzoli, 2020.

Jessen, Monique. "The Hidden Good-Luck Charm Sewn into the Queen's Coronation Gown—and 4 Other Secrets!" *People*. Last updated June 2, 2021. https://people.com/royals/queen-elizabeths-coronation-gown.

Kelly, Angela. *The Other Side of the Coin: The Queen, the Dresser and the Wardrobe*. New York: Harper, 2019.

Lacey, Robert. *Monarch: The Life & Reign of Elizabeth II*. New York: Free Press, 2002.

Lacey, Robert. *The Queen: A Life in Brief.* New York: Harper Perennial, 2012.

Lilley, Harvey, dir. *The Coronation.* London, United Kingdom: Atlantic Productions, BBC, 2018.

Morton, Andrew. *Elizabeth & Margaret: The Intimate World of the Windsor Sisters.* New York: Grand Central Publishing, 2021.

Murphy, Victoria. *Town & Country: The Queen: A Life in Pictures.* New York: Hearst Home, 2021.

Perry, Simon. "Queen Elizabeth and Princess Margaret on VE Day 1945." *People.* Last updated May 8, 2015. https://people.com/royals/queen-elizabeth-and-princess-margret-on-ve-day-1945.

Pimlott, Ben. *The Queen: A Biography of Elizabeth II.* Hoboken: Wiley, 1998.

"Prince Philip Has Died Aged 99, Buckingham Palace Announces." *BBC News.* April 9, 2021. https://www.bbc.com/news/uk-11437314.

"Prince Philip: Land Rover Hearse and Other Personal Touches at Duke's Funeral." *BBC News.* April 17, 2021. https://www.bbc.com/news/uk-56762822.

"Princess Anne Defends 'Caring' Queen." *BBC News.* April 29, 2002. http://news.bbc.co.uk/2/hi/uk_news/1958074.stm.

Rhodes, Margaret. *The Final Curtsey: A Royal Memoir by the Queen's Cousin.* Edinburgh: Birlinn Limited, 2012.

Silverman, Leah. "These Are All of Queen Elizabeth's Homes." *Town & Country.* November 12, 2020. https://www.townandcountrymag.com/leisure/real-estate/g14106752/queen-elizabeth-homes/.

Slavin, Rose. "50 Facts about The Queen's Coronation." *The Royal Family.* June 7, 2017. https://www.royal.uk/50-facts-about-queens-coronation-0.

Smith, Sally Bedell. *Elizabeth the Queen: The Life of a Modern Monarch.* New York: Random House, 2012.

Tonelli, Lucia. "Queen Elizabeth's Former Malta Villa Is on the Market for $6.7 Million." *Town & Country.* June 13, 2019. https://www.townandcountrymag.com/society/tradition/a28004050/queen-elizabeth-malta-villa-for-sale.

Trebay, Guy. "The Outfits That Say 'The Queen.'" *The New York Times.* June 1, 2012. https://www.nytimes.com/2012/06/03/fashion/queen-elizabeth-ii-sets-a-style-standard.html.

ABOUT THE AUTHORS

© Nicki Sebastian

Rachel Bowie is cohost of the _Royally Obsessed_ podcast, recently named one of the best podcasts of 2021 by _Town & Country_. She's also director of special projects for PureWow.com, a role that has led her to cover the royals—say, test driving Kate Middleton's go-to coat brand or penning an op-ed about Prince Harry and Meghan Markle's future beyond the Palace—for over six years. Her love of the royals was sealed at a young age following the death of Princess Diana, but also growing up as a mega-fan of Princes William and Harry—and subsequently Kate and Meghan.

© Kaitlin Simpson

Roberta Fiorito is cohost of the _Royally Obsessed_ podcast, recently named one of the best podcasts of 2021 by _Town & Country_. She's also senior editor of branded content at Gallery Media Group, and has covered the royal beat for PureWow.com for over five years, meticulously poring over every Meghan Markle sighting and Kate Middleton outfit choice. She's been a devotee of the royals ever since her family moved to Scotland for a year, where she was immersed in U.K. culture and history.